The Cornerstone
of Childbirth Education
Student Workbook:
The Muslim Edition

3rd Edition, 2017

THE CORNERSTONE METHOD OF CHILDBIRTH EDUCATION

ENGAGE. INFORM. EMPOWER.

Nickie Tilsner, CBE, CD, CHOW

Juli Tilsner, CBE, CPM, LM

With Nethal Abdul-Mu'min, CBE, CD, BA Islamic Studies

2

INTRODUCTION TO THE MUSLIM EDITION

We are delighted to offer Muslim families information about birth that supports their specific needs and is both empowering and complementary to their beliefs and values. You will find that we have included drawings and photographs that are modest and inclusive of all types of birthing Muslims. We have been sensitive to Islamic dietary laws, and integrated Islamic thikr into the easy to follow relaxation scripts (access the original scripts in Appendix C). Our hope is that all types of Muslims will feel comfortable using this book. If you have any suggestions for improvements in the book or instructional methods, please bring it to our attention.

RELIGION ADDENDUM

The Cornerstone Method and Cornerstone Doula Training is committed to expanding the access of representative childbirth education materials to all communities. Our dear friend, Nethal Abdul-Mu'min graciously offered to write the Muslim edition of our student workbook to help fill the great gap in educational materials that are available to our Muslim students. Cornerstone is not affiliated with any religion or religious group, and this workbook does not represent the beliefs of Cornerstone as an organization.

A NOTE ABOUT INCLUSIVITY

You may notice that we use many different terms and pronouns when referring to the person who gives birth, partner, and baby. When we use the terms birthing person, she/his/their, and chestfeeding, we are making a conscious effort to be inclusive to all who participate in our courses. We wish to honor any and all family structures, partnerships, and gender identities. The Cornerstone Method is intended to work for anyone, regardless of cultural background, religion, birth plan, chosen birth location, sexual identity, gender identity, and family structure. If you feel that there is a lack of inclusion in our language in any way, please contact the writers of this workbook at cornerstonedoulatrainings@gmail.com to bring this to our attention and we will revise as needed. We wish everyone an empowering and joyful birth experience.

TABLE OF CONTENTS

THE CORNERSTONE METHOD OF CHILDBIRTH EDUCATION

ENGAGE. INFORM. EMPOWER.

INTRODUCTION

INTRODUCTION

The Cornerstone Method prepares participants for birth by integrating **eight special birth senses:** Body Awareness, Sight, Sound, Breath, Touch, Smell, Voice, and Joy into your pregnancy, labor, birth, and beyond. Learn to work with all of these senses in preparation for and during the big event.

The senses:

Body Awareness: Understand the process of birth and all of the amazing changes that you will be encountering during pregnancy. Gain easy to use tools to care for yourself and your baby throughout the childbearing year.

Sight: Create your birth vision and map the route to its destination.

Sound: What you hear during pregnancy and birth affects the outcome.

Breath: Learn to use the breath for nourishment, relaxation, and pain relief.

Touch: Learn how to use touch and movement to relieve pain and discomfort.

Smell: Simple ways to use scents and aromatherapies to aide in easing nausea, exhaustion, and discomfort.

Voice: Speak up for your needs! Learn about how to ask questions of your care providers to get the information you need to make informed decisions.

Joy: Find freedom and joy in your body, pregnancy, and birth experience.

The information:

- Modern, evidence based, culturally inclusive, and thorough.

- Deepens the expecting family's understanding of their options with unbiased information to aide in making informed decisions.

- Demystifies pregnancy and birth with easy to understand descriptions of anatomy and physiology.

- Instills healthy habits during pregnancy with up to date nutrition and exercise instruction.

- Engages participants by using group exercises and games to enhance learning and community building.

- Prepares for varied birth scenarios in all settings.

- Enhances your understanding of the prenatal and post birth parent/baby connection and gives tools for deepening the bonding process.

QUESTIONS EXERCISE:

What questions did you come into your first class with? There are no irrelevant or wrong questions to ask. You may find during the pregnancy questions exercise that most other expecting parents have the same curiosities.

List three questions that the pregnant person came to this course with:

1:

2:

3:

List three questions that the partner or support person came to this course with:

1:

2:

3:

The next eight weeks will be a great exercise in exploration and learning. More questions will be revealed as time goes on, and it is recommended to keep track of these questions so they are fresh in your mind at the beginning of each class meeting.

CLASS ONE

SENSE: SMELL

FIRST TRIMESTER SURVIVAL TIPS

The first thing to understand about your first trimester discomforts is there is a reason you are nauseas and have food aversions. Don't make the nausea worse by trying to "eat your greens". Your appetite for vegetables will probably return by your 15th week. Exhaustion is experienced between approximately 4-12 weeks. This is when the pregnancy is establishing itself and your body is expending a lot of energy, wanting you to be down and resting. *Pushing through the exhaustion contributes to nausea and headaches.* Put your exercise regime on hold until the exhaustion lifts, allowing yourself to take the time your body needs to build a new human.

Now is the time to get used to staying hydrated. This will be a new habit that you will find is essential for pregnancy and breastfeeding/chest feeding. You now need about 2 liters of water per day, with added electrolytes. You also need to salt your food. Salt and electrolytes support your rapidly increasing blood supply and help prevent or lessen pregnancy headaches.

The most important piece of advice that we can give you about self-care in pregnancy is to trust your body. It will tell you what it needs. When the nausea, exhaustion and aversion to eating greens that you may have been experiencing lifts, that is your green light to get back to business as usual for the next phase of your pregnancy. We realize many people won't be able to take off work or school. If your life is hectic, try your best to schedule in 15-minute rest periods every 2-3 hours, which will help you get through the first trimester in a much more enjoyable and healthy way. It will also benefit your workplace by making it possible for you to come to work and not have to call in sick.

NAUSEA RECOMMENDATIONS

Check with care provider if your prenatal vitamins are causing nausea and digestive upset. Consider finding an alternative like an herbal infusion drink until the first trimester nausea lets up. It is good to remember that supplements are called supplements because they are to be used in addition to good nutrition. If your supplements are making you feel so sick that you cannot eat food, they will not be doing the job that you need them to. If you do find an alternative source of prenatal vitamins in the first trimester, we recommend staying on your Folate (folic acid is the pharmaceutical form) supplement until 12 weeks of pregnancy, when the neural tube is completely formed.

- Let yourself rest.

- Eat often, snacking every hour or two. Low blood sugar = nausea and headaches.

- Protein load: Eat some protein every hour.

- Keep snacks handy for middle of the night wakes. Try sips of smoothie, cheese sticks, ¼ of a nut butter sandwich and other easy to eat, simple snacks.
-
- Sea 'Acupressure' Wrist Bands. These are used for nausea caused by travel sickness and work for pregnancy induced nausea as well. Find them at your local drugstore.

- Treat yourself to acupuncture. Acupuncture can do wonders to help alleviate morning sickness ie: all day sickness for some! Many cities have community acupuncture clinics and Chinese Medicine school clinics. These clinics are low fee and sliding scale

YOUR OWN PERSONAL COMFORT FOODS ARE OFTEN WHAT YOU NEED.

- Baked potato / butter / sour cream

- Macaroni and cheese

- Toast with peanut butter and honey

- Oranges

- Bagels and cream cheese

- Smoothies with some fat and protein content: take a sip or two every hour to keep your stomach from going empty and to keep your blood sugar level.

- Lemonade (homemade or fresh, made from real lemons) add ginger (optional)

- Ginger: candies, teas, ginger syrup with honey, capsules

- Mint tea

- Popsicles made from any of the drinks listed, including smoothies.

REMEMBER

- Don't stress: You will not harm your baby if what you can keep down is limited for the first 12-15 weeks. *The health of the first trimester of pregnancy draws on the months before you even got pregnant.*

- Eat every 2 hours: Graze! Low blood sugar = nausea and headaches; even in the middle of the night!

- Eat a little protein with every 'meal' or snack. This way you will easily reach your protein goals each day.

PREGNANCY DISCOMFORTS 101

MORNING SICKNESS

Morning sickness is defined as nausea and vomiting any time of the day; it is not just limited to the morning hours. Usually this is limited to the first trimester, from approximately week 4 through 15. Hormonal changes and hypoglycemia are thought to be the main contributors to morning sickness. *See page 11-12 for nausea recommendations.*

HEADACHES

Headaches are common in the first trimester due to changes in the circulatory system. They are also common if you have quit caffeine cold turkey, which many people do when they find out they are pregnant. If you are in pain from caffeine withdraw, consider letting yourself have one weak cup of organic coffee or tea per day, weaning yourself off over the period of a week or two. If you have headaches and migraines when you are not pregnant, there is a chance you may have a bothersome increase in early pregnancy. Take preventative measures by listening to your body. Do not push yourself to do more than you have energy for and take naps often. Do not let yourself get low on blood sugar; try to snack frequently, every 1-2 hours. Stay hydrated by keeping up with water and electrolyte drink intake and be sure to stay away from drinks that are full of processed sugars, artificial sweeteners and colors. Electrolyte drinks are also sometimes called sports drinks. Making your own electrolyte drink is easy and economical. See page 18 for more on hydration.

CONSTIPATION

Constipation often occurs in early pregnancy due to slowing of the digestive system. The body has an increased need for hydration, which results in dry hard stool, and iron supplements can also be a culprit. Stay hydrated and if you are taking iron supplements, consider taking a food-based brand that your body can more easily digest. A very good example is "Floradix iron and herbs" that comes in liquid or pill form. You can try eating 3-6 dried apricots and/ or prunes each day, and steamed or roasted beets can also be very effective.

HEMORRHOIDS AND VARICOSE VEINS

Veins that are distended and swollen can be a result of expanded blood volume and progesterone, which dilate the veins. Most times this is temporary, though some vessels that have lost their elasticity will remain visible after pregnancy. Legs are the most common area to experience this discomfort, and rarely there are vulvar varicosities. Hemorrhoids are varicose veins of the rectum. In pregnancy, your body releases hormones that relax smooth muscle, soften ligaments and the cartilage in your pelvis, and relax the blood vessels. This vessel relaxation, as well as the added weight and pressure from the pregnancy can sometimes cause hemorrhoids. Most hemorrhoids and varicose veins will shrink significantly within three months post birth, not continuing to give you problems. Staying hydrated is paramount in hemorrhoid prevention, as straining from constipation is a risk factor for their development. Using a foot-stool, which puts you in a squatting style position while moving your bowels is a healthy life habit that can greatly aid in prevention.

Other Preventative measures for vein health:

- 500-1000mg Vitamin C with bioflavanoids every day to help strengthen blood vessels - *unless you have a condition that would bar you from this supplementation.*
- Avoid sitting or standing in one position for long periods of time, which takes pressure off of your bottom and keeps circulation moving.
- Get regular exercise
- Elevate your legs periodically through the day

BLEEDING GUMS

Bleeding gums when brushing and flossing are also a side effect of your hormonal changes and blood volume increase, which makes the gums slightly softer and puffy. Taking 500-1000mg Vit. C with bioflavanoids daily will help alleviate this problem.

HEARTBURN

Heartburn affects most pregnant people at some point during the pregnancy as a result of elevated progesterone levels. This hormone relaxes smooth muscle in pregnancy, but also relaxes the stomach valve that keeps acid out of the esophagus. In addition, the growing uterus crowds the stomach, which forces acid into the esophagus.
Some tricks that may help to alleviate the burn:

- Limit what you drink with meals. Liquid dilutes your digestive juices, and can lengthen digestion time. The food then 'ferments' more in your stomach, causing gastric upset.

- Take a walk after meals; even a short walk around the block will aid in digestion.

- Take digestive enzymes to support efficient digestion. Try Papaya enzymes or a combination digestive enzyme tablet rather than Tums, as these enzymes work more naturally with your body's digestion and do not have any harmful side effects.

LEG CRAMPS

"Charley horses" are common in pregnancy and they usually occur during the night, waking you from sleep.

- Try getting an added serving of calcium/magnesium before bed.

- Make sure you are hydrated and have consumed enough salt every day.

- Take an epsom salt bath before bed. Use 1-2 cups of salts in your bath for the best effect; also helping you have a good night's sleep.

LOWER BACK PAIN

Your growing uterus exerts a downward and forward pull on the lower spine that can lead to lower back aches and pain. Another contributing factor is the pregnant body's release of the hormone relaxin, which results in loose ligaments, making your joints less stable and more easily stressed. This is more common in late pregnancy, but can happen any time.
Lower back pain can be alleviated and possibly avoided altogether by following the simple steps of optimal fetal positioning, which are outlined later in this chapter.

Prevention and coping strategies:

- Proper posture and pelvic alignment

- Chiropractic care

- Ergonomic seating devices and bolsters

- Pillows for support while sleeping and resting

- Swimming

- Prenatal yoga

- Cat cow yoga pose or pelvic tilts throughout the day.

SHORTNESS OF BREATH

Mild breathlessness and feeling winded are common in pregnancy.
Once again, hormones are hard at work, changing your body's physiology to support both you and baby. First trimester hormones relax your lung muscles and bronchial tubes, making you have to actually work to fill the lungs. Shortness of breath in the second trimester is a result of your brain being stimulated to increase the frequency and depth of your breaths, allowing you to take in more oxygen for you and baby. In the third trimester the baby gets larger and puts pressure on your diaphragm, which makes less room for your lungs to fully expand. Great news: towards the final weeks or days, your baby will start the journey downward and drop into the pelvis, giving you a reprieve from this feeling, as there is now more room for your lungs to expand.

BREAST CHANGES

This can be one of the first signs you are pregnant. Your breast changes are caused by a surge of hormones that stimulate the growth of milk ducts. First time moms experience these symptoms more dramatically than multiparas (those who have been pregnant before). You may feel soreness, swelling, tingling, increase in warmth, throbbing sensations, and sensitivity to touch. The soreness usually lets up in the second trimester. Your areolas may enlarge and darken in color and the veins in your breasts become more noticeable. You may or may not experience a wet sticky fluid leaking from the ducts in your areola. Although this is very exciting, no need to worry if it doesn't happen until labor and birth. Expect your breast size to increase 2 sizes by the end of the pregnancy, but know that some women do not experience an enlargement of breast tissue and go on to have normal milk production. If you are nursing a little one when you get pregnant, you will most likely have the initial soreness, and may not want to be touched for a while. Early in the pregnancy, your milk will also go through changes and your nursing counterpart may notice a decrease in volume and a change in flavor. This might lead to a voluntary end to nursing or being satisfied with nursing only for comfort through the changes. You will also be deciding what is right for both of you on a day-to-day basis. Remember, breastfeeding is a relationship; it needs to work for both participants!

INCREASED URINATION

The hormones of pregnancy along with the growing uterus pressing against your bladder will send you to the restroom frequently in the first trimester. You will get some relief in the second trimester when the uterus rises out of the pelvis and takes the pressure off. Because of the extra fluid you need to be taking in and putting out on a daily basis, you will get used to urinating more often than you did in non-pregnant life. Toward the end of the pregnancy, when baby drops into the pelvis you will find yourself planning your days around where bathrooms are closest!

ROUND LIGAMENT PAIN

Two uterine supporting ligaments are located on the left and right side of your uterus and attach to the groin, or 'inguinal' area. As the uterus grows, these ligaments stretch and can cramp. The sensations can be quite a shock, but only last seconds up to a couple minutes in length. You may feel twitches, as well as sharp or cramping pain on either side of your lower belly and/or groin. Some of the movements that can bring on this cramping are coughing, laughing or standing up too quickly. If you know that you are going to sneeze, cough, or laugh you can bend and flex your hips, which can reduce the pull on the ligaments. When you feel these sensations, lean into them and breathe. It should subside very quickly. If there is lingering pain, a hot water bottle or warm bath can be soothing. If you experience pain that does not go away with breathing, stretching, and heat, contact your care provider.

WHY AM I TOLD NOT TO LIE ON MY BACK?

After 20 weeks, a small percentage of women feel dizzy or nauseas when they lie on their backs. The weight of your uterus and baby can occlude blood flow to the upper half of your body and lower your blood pressure by compressing the inferior vena cava (major blood vessels in your abdomen). This sounds really scary, but there is really no way you can hurt yourself or your baby, as your body will respond to the lowered blood pressure with dizziness and or nausea. Your body will wake you up from sleep to have you change positions if you need. The key is, listen to your body when it speaks to you. If lying on your back feels fine, then it is! *Please note that if you are taking medications that impair perception, alcohol, or drugs you may not get these messages from your body to change positions or wake up. If you are using any of these, it is a good idea* **not** *to lie on your back.*

NUTRITIONAL TIPS

Eat whole foods as much as possible, limiting the processed foods that you consume. Always choose whole fat, which will keep your energy up and assist in maintaining a healthy metabolism. Whole fat foods are more filling and satisfying; you will eat less and stay satiated longer. Most people don't know that low fat food products are altered making them unrecognizable to our bodies, and we have a hard time processing and assimilating them. A common side effect of eating low fat foods is lactose intolerance.

Every body is different: Protein needs increase with gestation.
Your body will guide you on how much protein to eat. The right amount for you on any given day will make you feel good and strong.

FOR MOST PEOPLE, THESE AMOUNTS ARE RECOMMENDED:

- First trimester 40-60 grams

- Second trimester 60-75 grams

- Third trimester 75-100 grams

For multiples add 300-500 calories and 20-30 grams of protein a day for each additional baby. *An easier way to think about this is to add 2-4 more snacks through the day.* We crave sweets when we are low on calories because our body wants a quick blood sugar fix. Eat a well-balanced snack, before reaching for that sweetie and you will find that you feel more satisfied and won't suffer a blood sugar crash, which includes nausea and headaches.

SOME SNACK IDEAS

- Apple slices and nuts or nut butter

- Apple slices and cheese

- Carrots and hummus

- Whole grain bread, topped with avocado

- Deviled eggs

- Corn chips with whole milk yogurt and salsa mixed together as a dip

- Banana and nuts

- See our recipes for some easy, nutritious snacks

When buying pre-made protein bars, make sure there is a protein to carbohydrate ratio of no less than 50%. This will sustain you longer, without a blood sugar spike, and crash.
Common examples are: Protein 7g/carb 14gm, protein 20 gm/carb 40 gm (or less).

Energy bars are for quick energy and are high in carbs, low in protein. They are good for consuming before strenuous exercise, but are not made to substitute meals. *Always make sure to have a balanced snack with protein right after your workout.*

If you do eat protein or nutritional bars, make sure to consume those with the least amount of ingredients; as close to whole foods as you can get.   Whole foods are always better for your body than a processed snack bar. Bars are great for food 'emergencies'. I suggest always having one in your bag or car, for the event you have gone too long without food and need something to get you through.

HYDRATION

Stay hydrated by keeping up with water, herbal tea, and electrolyte intake. Try to stay away from drinks that are full of sugar, processed or artificial sweeteners & artificial colors. Electrolyte drinks are often called sports drinks. The general recommendation for fluid intake is about 2 liters per day. Making your own electrolyte drink is easy and economical. The foundation of a good electrolyte drink is simply lemon or limeade made with a natural sweetener of choice and sea salt to taste. Unrefined sea salt offers many of the trace minerals that are added to store bought electrolyte drinks. There are many fun and delicious recipes to find online. Mix it up. A general guideline is to get about 50% of your fluid intake with electrolytes. Follow your body's cues. If you find that water alone is not quenching your thirst, your body may be asking for electrolytes and salt. Electrolytes help hold the fluid you are drinking in your bloodstream, and cells instead of some going straight through and peeing it out. Your baby benefits as hydration also has some effect on amniotic fluid levels. It can also help you not have to urinate so often!

SALT

Salt food to taste and do not avoid salt, unless you have a condition or disease state in which your healthcare provider has you on a low salt diet. If you are having a healthy pregnancy and craving salt, eat more! Salt supports your body in many ways, including your expanding blood volume and amniotic fluid. Unrefined Sea Salt has naturally occurring minerals and iodine, but less iodine than table salt. *Table salt has been stripped of trace minerals and enriched with pharmaceutical iodine and anti-caking agents such as aluminum and silicon dioxide.*
 Iodine is an essential nutrient for optimal thyroid function. The Institute of Medicine "IOM" recommends 220 mcg. per day for pregnancy and 290 mgs. per day for breastfeeding/chest feeding people. If you eat fish, dairy and sea salt, you are most likely getting enough of your daily requirement.
If you are vegan, you can get your iodine from some foods, although to stay in the range you may want to check on the amount of iodine in your prenatal vitamin. If they do not have the daily amount required, talk to your provider or a nutritionist about the best way to meet your iodine needs.

GET YOUR VITAMIN D LEVELS CHECKED.

According to Dr. Sears "Having a Healthy Pregnancy", Low levels of maternal vitamin D are associated with:

- Increased C section rates

- More allergies in baby

- Weaker bones in baby and person who gave birth

Always strive for great nutrition. You will have really good days and not so great days, and this ok! Your nutrition intake will all balance out. Be free to enjoy your pregnancy and the food you eat. Being conscious of what you eat forms new good eating habits for life, which will be passed on to your baby and new family.

PROTEIN

"Since the entire structure of your baby's body, including her/his brain, will be largely made from the protein you eat, your first concern must be to obtain adequate protein of high quality. You will also require protein to keep your own muscles, vital organs, and other tissues in constant repair, to produce hormones, enzymes, antibodies and blood cells for yourself, and to form new tissues in your uterus and breasts." Adelle Davis, 'Let's have Healthy Children'

When proteins are digested, they are broken down into amino acids. Amino Acids are the building blocks for all body structures. 10-12 amino acids can be built within the body, but 8-10 amino acids must be supplied by your diet, which is why they are called "essential". As well as building your body's structures, the protein that you eat feeds your liver, keeping it healthy, so that it can produce a serum protein called albumin. When you don't have enough protein in your diet, albumin levels fall which causes water to be taken from the bloodstream into certain areas of the body: hands, feet, ankles, and face. This is called edema. Edema is different than the healthy swelling that you will see in your hands and feet, which is a side effect of your normal expanding blood supply. When you have edema from low protein levels, albumin is also taken out of the bloodstream along with the water, and will eventually leave the body in your urine. When your healthcare provider checks your urine and there is no protein present, it is a sign that your metabolic systems are healthy and that you are eating enough protein. Conversely, if protein is present in your urine, it may mean that you need to consume more protein. If your provider finds protein in your urine, he or she may run more tests to see if your body is metabolically stable and that your liver is functioning properly. As well as the swelling and metabolic issues that can be a result of not getting enough protein in your diet, your vital organs are also at risk; particularly your kidneys. Ineffective kidney function allows other important nutrients to leave the body in your urine before they can adequately nourish your body. When many of your vital organs cannot function correctly, your urine is not collected, so the unfiltered water is left in the body and results in more edema. This could be the beginning of pre-eclampsia, which is a serious problem in pregnancy. High blood pressure and extreme edema are symptoms of pre-eclampsia and can result in the need for an induced delivery of the baby, no matter how many weeks you have left. Pre-eclampsia is a condition that in the later stages, is called eclampsia or Toxemia.

Warning signs of pre-eclampsia and toxemia include: extreme edema especially of hands, face and chest, protein in the urine (proteinuria), extreme headache that won't resolve, visual disturbances (seeing spots), right upper gastric pain/pain in the liver, and high blood pressure.

Not eating enough protein is one of the *possible* causes of this condition. Some research points to Calcium/ Magnesium deficiency as also being a risk factor, but there is still a lot that is unknown about the causes of pre-eclampsia and eclampsia. No matter how you look at it, a strong body with well-nourished organs is more likely to remain healthy throughout the pregnancy and birth. Pregnancy increases a person's protein requirements to up to 75-100 grams of protein per day. It is possible to eat too much protein, although it is very hard to do so. If you are striving for 90-100 grams a day and it is making you feel run down, heavy, nauseous, or just plain bad, then try lowering your protein a bit until you find the right amount for your body. Protein requirements start lower in the early months and increase throughout the duration of the pregnancy.

If you feel run down and have bouts of low blood sugar, try resolving by eating little snacks with protein every 2 hours throughout the day. This is actually a very healthy way to eat in general. There is an excellent chapter on nutrition in "The Healthy Pregnancy Book" by Dr. Sears.

GOOD EXAMPLES OF BLOOD SUGAR STABILIZING SNACKS

- Apple slices and a slice or two of hard cheese.

- Apple slices and a handful of roasted nuts or nut butter (without added sugar)

- Carrots and bell pepper slices with hummus

- Carrots and almond butter

- Celery and nut butter with raisins on top (ants on a log)

- Plain Greek yogurt, a little fresh fruit, nuts and chia seeds. Add some blackstrap molasses to sweeten, also adding calcium and iron.

- Sliced Turkey or Salami, pickles, and a few corn chips

- Whole grain toast with avocado and cheese

- Scrambled eggs with whole grain toast

FATS

Did you know that your baby's brain is 60% Fat?

Good Fat/Bad Fat
The government guidelines on fat consumption have recently been updated to say YES to cholesterol and good fats, including Omega 3's.

The fats and oils that were thought to be healthy fats, primarily vegetable oils derived from soy, corn, safflower, cottonseed, and canola are now proving to contribute to a large number of diseases, weight gain, and an excess of omega 6 and 3 deficiencies. These oils are **polyunsaturated**, and tend to become oxidized or rancid, carrying free radicals and causing damage to our cells when subjected to heat, oxygen and moisture.
*Cottonseed: one of the most pesticide laden.

It is a known fact that heavy metals and toxins are stored in fat. Animals that eat or are exposed to these toxins and chemicals store them in their fat cells, and these chemicals end up in our food supply. When eating dairy, meat, and fish, go organic, grass fed, pasture raised, and wild as much as possible. Grass fed butter is easy to find in the grocery. Grass fed butter is a super food: full of antioxidants, good cholesterol, and vit K2, which decalcifies arteries. Coconut butter contains lauric acid to boost the immune system and medium chain triglycerides, which are fats that act like carbohydrates. These triglycerides metabolize directly in the liver and give us more energy per gram consumed.

HEALTHY FATS

Saturated fats are solid at room temperature and are highly stable by their chemical makeup. **They do not easily go rancid or form free radicals when heated for cooking purposes.**

SATURATED

- Butter
- Coconut
- Prepared animal fats such as ghee, schmaltz, duck fat.

These fats are staples in traditional diets. Often they are prepared by a process called rendering. They are melted and clarified which removes the food solids from the fat. This makes these fats very stable and will last a long time without going rancid. It is optimal to use fats from animals raised as naturally as possible to minimize exposure to pesticides and antibiotic residues.

MONOUNSATURATED (relatively stable, do not go rancid easily)

- Oils from pecans, almonds, cashews, peanuts, olive, and avocado.

The Healthy Pregnancy Book, by William and Martha Sears says:
"Pregnant and breastfeeding mothers should eat 12 oz. of safe seafood per week.
Take 500mg. of omega-3 DHA/EPA fish oil supplements daily to reach the goal of 1000 mg (1 gram) per day. If not eating seafood, take at least 1000mg omega-3 DHA/EPA daily. At least 600 mg. Should be omega-3 DHA...Research shows that mothers who eat more safe seafood or take omega 3 fish oil supplements during pregnancy and for 3 months post delivery:

- Are less likely to suffer pre and postpartum depression

- Have a lower chance of delivering a premature baby or less than optimal birth weight

- Have babies who are more likely to have better visual acuity

- Have children who are less likely to develop skin and respiratory allergies

- Have children who are more likely to have higher IQs

"...go organic for dairy. The last thing you and your growing baby need is a bunch of "endocrine disrupters," the term now used to describe the possible harmful effects of hormones and other pharmaceuticals given to dairy cows." - Dr. Sears

CHOLESTEROL

" Your baby's growing body and brain-as well as yours-needs extra cholesterol. Cholesterol is one of the top brain fats in growing your little "fathead" and you need additional cholesterol to make the pregnancy maintaining hormones progesterone and estrogen."
Dr. Sears, The Healthy Pregnancy Book.

From Nourishing Traditions, by Sally Fallon:

- Cholesterol is a precursor to Vitamin D, a fat-soluble vitamin needed for healthy bones and nervous system, proper growth, mineral metabolism, muscle tone, **insulin production,** and reproduction and immune system function.

- Bile salts are made from cholesterol. Bile is vital for digestion and assimilation of dietary fats.

- Cholesterol is needed for proper function of serotonin receptors in the brain. Serotonin is the body's natural 'feel good' chemical. Low cholesterol levels have been linked to aggressive and violent behavior, as well as depression.

- Mother's milk is especially rich in cholesterol and contains a special enzyme that helps the baby utilize this nutrient. Babies and children need cholesterol-rich foods throughout their growing years to ensure proper development of their brain and nervous system.

Research has never established any clear relationship between the consumption of dietary cholesterol and the risk for heart disease.

EAT EGGS!

Egg yolks are an excellent source of cholesterol and they have a built in component called lecithin that helps you metabolize the fats in the yolk. A rule of thumb: the darker orange color of the yolk, the more nutritious it is. You will find beautiful color to the yolks in pastured eggs, where the birds are subject to sunlight, fresh air, and can roam and eat bugs. To satisfy the government's modest daily recommendation, you need to eat 4 yolks. Egg whites are a perfect protein and egg yolks provide: choline (brain neuron development), vitamins A,D,E,K, biotin, iron, zinc, selenium and folate.

*In a study conducted by Mother Earth News, folate levels were over 200 times higher in pastured eggs than in eggs from chickens raised in confinement.

NOTES:

OTHER FOODS THAT CONTAIN CHOLESTEROL

- Heavy Cream
- Butter
- Duck
- Salmon
- Beef
- Lamb
- Turkey
- Sardines
- Crab
- Shrimp
- Liver
- Giblets & Brains

VITAMINS AND MINERALS:

FOLIC ACID VS. FOLATE

It is recommended that all non-pregnant people of childbearing age take 400- 800 micrograms per day of 'Folic Acid' to prevent neural tube defects, in the event of pregnancy. While pregnant, it is recommended to supplement 800 micrograms per day for the first 12 weeks, until the neural tube is completely developed. Most prenatal vitamins have 800 mcg. folic acid, and you can find this information on the bottle's nutritional facts.

This is a good example of synthetic vs. food-based supplements.
Folic Acid is synthetic folate. Folic Acid is added to processed foods, which is called "fortification" or "fortified". You will find that many breads, cereals, and crackers are fortified. Some new research is showing that many people cannot metabolize this synthetic form, causing risk for health problems, especially folic acid anemia. Folate is the natural form found in many foods, including spinach and liver. There are now many health- conscious companies that manufacture food based supplements, and they can be found at most natural food stores. Be sure to look for Folate in your prenatal vitamins.

VITAMIN C WITH BIOFLAVANOIDS

Vitamin C is an essential component of collagen, the most abundant protein in the body that is essential for building new bone, cartilage, tendon, skin, other connective tissue, membranes, and strengthens capillary and blood vessel walls. In pregnancy terms, this essential element will help make a strong bag of waters, prevent or lessen bleeding gums, bloody nose (small amount of pink on tissue after blowing nose), and varicose veins including hemorrhoids. It will also aid in healing after the birth. Some midwives recommend their clients supplement 500-1000 mg. Vit.C with bioflavonoids daily. Any food that contains vitamin C also contains bioflavonoids. Bioflavonoids are required for absorption of vitamin C and both work together in the body.

Some foods that bioflavonoids are found in:
Citrus fruit rinds and pulp, apples, buckwheat, berries, red pepper, hot chili's, broccoli,parsley, kale, brussels sprouts, kiwi, melon, papaya.

When purchasing a supplement, look for the most bioavailable form such as Ester-C, and/or mineral ascorbates rather than ascorbic acid. Mineral ascorbates (also known as buffered) are usually much gentler on the gastrointestinal system.If the amount you are taking is causing loose bowels, reduce to your personal bowel tolerance.

IRON

Iron is the key ingredient in hemoglobin, which is a component of red blood cells. Hemoglobin acts as a carrier of oxygen from the lungs to the tissues, and aids in the removal of carbon dioxide from the tissues, allowing it to be released from the body when we breathe out. Hemoglobin gives blood its healthy red color and without hemoglobin to carry oxygen to the tissues, our cells would die. Hemoglobin, many enzymes, and a substance called myoglobin which carries oxygen within our muscle cells, cannot be produced without iron. Iron is used up constantly by our bodies in varying degrees and needs to be continually replaced through what we eat. A pregnant woman has an expanding blood volume and needs more iron. Dietary iron is necessary for fetal development, including the baby's own iron stores, as well as maternal anemia prevention in both pregnant and nursing people, and replacement of their blood lost at birth. Only a small amount of iron consumed is actually utilized and maximizing absorption in addition to increasing intake is key in obtaining the amount of iron needed in pregnancy. When iron consumption and absorption are low, iron deficiency anemia may result. Feeling tired all the time, even with adequate rest, is the most common sign. Other symptoms may include paleness, tired aching muscles, headache, dizziness, and shortness of breath, all of which are symptoms of insufficient oxygenation of the cells. Please note that increased risk of infection and emotional depression can also result from iron deficiency anemia.

WHILE PREGNANT, YOU WILL NEED 30-60 MG OF IRON DAILY.

- Add extra iron to your meal and cook in high quality cast iron, especially when cooking acidic foods like tomato sauce.

- Regular aerobic exercise improves iron absorption, due to the body's greater need for oxygen carrying capacity.

- Choose iron supplements carefully. Food based supplements are absorbed and utilized much better than pharmaceutical iron supplements. Floradix Iron and Herbs, and World Organics liquid iron and herbs are two examples of food based, bio-available supplements.

- If you get constipated and/or your stool gets very dark or black, then you are not assimilating the iron. Find a different source.

- Iron supplements are best taken with food. This slows movement through the digestive tract, which increases absorption.

- Pregnant women find iron supplements more tolerable if taken with the evening meal, when blood sugar is less likely to be low causing less likelihood of nausea.

- One cup of Pregnancy Tea blend, or just plain nettle tea made as an **infusion**, is one serving of iron, calcium, and magnesium.

- Infusion instructions: one handful of dried herb into 1 quart of boiling hot water. Turn off heat. Cover and steep for 4 hours or more. This makes the tea a nutritional beverage that is well utilized by most bodies. *See page 25 for infusion recipe.*

CALCIUM

Calcium is a mineral needed in larger quantities during pregnancy and breastfeeding. Note that a pregnant or nursing/chestfeeding person needs about 1200-2000 mg of calcium daily.

Calcium is important for the growth and strengthening of baby's bones, as well as the pregnant person's bones and teeth. Adequate calcium intake aides in preventing osteoporosis later in life, is essential for well functioning muscles and nerves, and helps with blood clotting.

Consider adding extra calcium/magnesium if you experience persistent leg cramping or difficulty sleeping, especially in the last weeks of pregnancy. Make sure to get a high quality food based form of calcium and/or magnesium supplement (if you are supplementing) that your body can fully digest and use. These food-based supplements can be found at any natural food store. Your prenatal vitamins should already contain calcium, so take a look at the bottle's nutrition facts to see how much you are getting in a day. Red raspberry leaf, red clover, nettles, and mint are herbs that are high in calcium and are recommended as a nutritional drink in pregnancy. To make an infusion, Steep 1 handful of herbs to one quart of water in a covered pot or jar for a minimum of 4 hours. You can drink them hot or cold throughout the day. Just like iron, vitamin C aids in calcium absorption. Also note that coffee, sugar, alcohol, processed iodized salt, and lack of exercise depletes calcium in our bodies.

NON-DAIRY CALCIUM RICH FOODS

- Blackstrap Molasses

- Sesame Seeds: tahini

- Garbanzo beans: hummus

- Chia Seeds

- Almonds

- Rhubarb

- Seaweed

- Collards

- Spinach

- Kale

- Broccoli

- Sweet Potato

- Quinoa

- Great Northern Beans

- White Beans

- Black eyed Peas

- Oranges and tangerines

- Salmon (with skin and bones ex: canned)

- Sardines (with skin and bones)

- Eggs

- Figs

- Dates Bonus: Dates eaten the last 4 weeks are linked to shorter labors!

NOTES:

FOOD AND DRINK RECIPES
Get protein, calcium, fat & omegas here!

HERBAL TEA INFUSION RECIPE FOR PREGNANCY

An infusion is a nutritional beverage. The herbs are steeped for 4 hours or more to extract the vitamins and minerals into the tea. One cup of the infusion is approximately one serving of calcium, iron and has many other essential trace minerals. For more information on herbal infusions, herbs during pregnancy and nutritional values we recommend www.herblore.com.

INGREDIENTS:
*Organic Herbs Recommended

Nettle Leaf: Nourishing, blood builder, kidney and Adrenal Support, energizing
Red Raspberry Leaf: Uterine tonic, high in vitamin C, E, calcium, iron, potassium, and minerals

Optional:

- Peppermint, Calcium/magnesium

- Spearmint, Calcium/magnesium

- Dandelion: Liver and kidney support

- Oatstraw: Nervine

- Lavender: Nervine

- Lemon balm: Nervine, flavonoids

- Rose Petals: Relaxing, antioxidants

- Rose Hips: Vitamin C, flavonoids

- Hibiscus: Vitamin C, anti-inflammatory

- Alfalfa: Vitamin K

INSTRUCTIONS:

- Before bed boil 4 ½ cups of water in a covered stainless steel saucepan

- Remove from heat

- Add 1 ounce dried herbs (that's a big, over-sized handful)

- Stir, cover and let sit overnight. (4 hours minimum)

- In the morning strain into a quart jar, then refrigerate.

- Drink cold, room temp or warm.

- Drink throughout the day.

- This counts towards your daily water goal.

CORNERSTONE'S FABULOUS NUT MILK RECIPE

- 1 cup organic raw nut or seed, such as cashew, hazelnut, almond, or sunflower.

- 1 pinch sea salt

- 1 tsp. vanilla (optional)

- 1-2 dates, maple syrup or other sweetener (optional)

Soak nuts in water 7 - 12 hours. Drain, rinse, and add to 4 cups water. Put in blender on high for one minute. Put blended nuts and water in refrigerator to sit for a few hours, which will extract more fat and protein into the water to make the CREAMIEST nut milk you have ever had! Use a fine mesh strainer to strain nut-meat out of the water, pressing out as much liquid as you can to get all of the good fat. Add salt, vanilla, and sweetener. (we like just a pinch of salt and vanilla.) You will end up with one quart of highly nutritious nut milk. The cost of making this at home is in most cases equivalent to a store bought carton of nut milk, but will contain the fat, protein, calcium, and enzymes that are missing from store bought, processed nut milks.

ANOTHER EASY WAY TO MAKE NUT MILK

- 1 tbsp. nut butter

- 1 cup water

- 1 small or ½ large date.

(To make horchata, add a bit of cinnamon!)
Mix together in blender and blend on high until creamy.

LEMON OR LIME ELECTROLYTE DRINK

Home made electrolyte drink or 'Labor Aid'
Drink any time, not just for labor!
Cost effective, beneficial for the whole family.

- 4 cups filtered water.
- 1/2 cup freshly squeezed lemon juice, lime juice or combo.
- 1/4 teaspoon celtic, himalayan or other non refined sea salt (packed with trace minerals)
- Add preferred unrefined sweetener to taste: IE: honey, maple syrup, agave, coconut sugar, or organic raw sugar (organic blackstrap molasses can add minerals as well)

COCONUT CHIA PUDDING

- 13.5 oz. water
- 1 can (13.5 oz) of organic full fat coconut milk
- ⅓ cup of chia seeds
- 1 tsp -1tbsp. raw honey, raw agave, or maple syrup to sweeten
- 1 tsp. Vanilla
- Toasted coconut flakes for garnish (optional)

Whisk water and coconut milk together until well combined. Stir in chia seeds, sweetener, vanilla, and optional powdered spices. Let stand an hour, stir again and refrigerate.

- Top with fruit
- Variation: Chai spice pudding, add powdered spices:
  ¾ tsp. Cinnamon, ½ tsp. cardamom,¼ tsp. Ginger, ⅛ tsp. clove,⅛ tsp. nutmeg.

CHOCOLATE AVOCADO COCONUT MILK PUDDING

- 1 ½ Ripe avocado, peeled and flesh removed from pit
- ⅓ cup raw organic cacao powder
- ⅓ cup maple syrup
- ¼ cup full fat coconut milk
- 2 tsp. vanilla
- Blend until creamy and eat straight from blender or chilled
- Makes 4, ¼ cup servings

http://www.inspirededibles.ca/2012/10/chocolate-avocado-pudding-with-coconut.html (great read on health benefits)

GRAIN AND GLUTEN FREE MUFFINS

http://wholelifestylenutrition.com/recipes/appetizers-snacks/the-easiest-gluten-free-and-grain-free-muffin-recipe-ever/
Serves: 12 muffins or 24 mini muffins
Ingredients

- 1 cup nut butter

- 2 medium sized bananas (The more ripe, the sweeter!

- 2 large eggs

- 1 teaspoon vanilla (try making your own!)

- 1- 2 tablespoons of honey or other sweetener such as maple syrup, agave, etc.)

- ½ teaspoon baking soda

- 1 teaspoon apple cider vinegar

Toppings: dehydrated unsweetened coconut flakes, raisins, flaxseed, dark chocolate chips, cinnamon, and/or anything else you can think of. I added even more tupelo honey ;) Feel free to lather on apple butter, strawberry preserves, or even more peanut butter. Ever heard of carrot jam? It's very tasty with this snack, too!

Instructions:

1. Preheat oven to 400 degrees F.

2. Place all ingredients into a blender or food processor. You can also use a stick blender if you have one.

3. Blend until well mixed.

4. Pour batter into a greased muffin tin. You can also use a mini muffin tin to make 24 mini muffins.

5. Add additional toppings of your choice to each muffin and lightly stir into each cup

6. Cook time: 15 minutes for full size muffins and 10 minutes for mini muffins.

7. Reheat in a toaster oven for about 4 minutes at 350 degrees F, or eat at room temperature.

LABOR SMOOTHIE

This is a wonderful way to get calories and energy in late labor.
Coconut milk is easily absorbed into the bloodstream, and most birthing people's bodies will say YES to it when everything else is a NO.

- One can whole fat, organic coconut milk.

- 2-3 Dates

- Fruit if desired - Fresh or frozen.

- Put all ingredients into blender and blend on high to puree and enjoy.

LIST SOME OF YOUR FAVORITE HEALTHY RECIPES HERE:

ARTICLES BY OUR FABULOUS DOULAS AND CHILDBIRTH EDUCATORS:

HEALTH AT EVERY SIZE IN PREGNANCY by Asiyah Abdul-Mu'min, Bay Area CCBE
www.transitionsbirthclasses.com

America is fat-phobic. Wherever we turn, we hear of the dangers of being overweight and the obesity epidemic. This bias permeates our culture and influences our beliefs about things like physical beauty and medicine. We label people as "overweight" or "obese" according to the BMI (Body Mass Index), then call them dangerously unhealthy. We assume they are personally responsible for their lot, that they must be lazy and eat poorly. When a person who is "too big" according to the BMI becomes pregnant, instead of meeting with smiles and congratulations, they are often shamed and met with fear, blame, and condemnation. The message is: it is one thing to do this to yourself, but how could you inflict your negligence on this innocent unborn child? Pregnant, large-bodied people are often put into the high-risk category just because they are large. They are subjected to more tests and procedures during pregnancy and more interventions during birth. However, a large body is not a "risk factor" during pregnancy. Risk factors in pregnancy are things like high blood pressure and diabetes. The majority of large-bodied pregnant people are healthy and can have healthy uncomplicated pregnancies and births.

The BMI (Body Mass Index) chart is the standard way for determining if a person is at a healthy weight or not. However, it is a fundamentally flawed measure because it does not take into account any information except height and weight. It does not care about gender, bone density, muscle mass, ethnicity, physical activity, family history, or eating habits. Research has repeatedly shown that health is not a number on a scale or chart; people of every shape and size can be healthy, just as people of every shape and size can be unhealthy. Body shape and size is determined largely by genetics. Health is determined largely by life style.

Large bodied pregnant people are often told to restrict weight gain during pregnancy. Sometimes, they are even advised to lose weight. This advice is dangerous. Restricting normal weight gain during pregnancy can deprive the growing baby of essential nutrients. That, in turn, *can* lead to health concerns for the pregnant person and the baby during pregnancy and birth, such as premature labor, low birth weight babies, and postpartum hemorrhage. Furthermore, dieting itself can lead to health problems. Studies show that approximately 95% of people who lose weight on a diet regain it, usually with a few more pounds. This is called weight cycling, or yo-yo dieting. Yo-yo dieting is very hard on the body and organs. It increases the risk of damaged arteries, heart disease, cancer, and diabetes. It is much healthier to stay large than to weight cycle.

The best way for a large-bodied pregnant person to have a healthy pregnancy and birth is for them to care for their body with love and respect, feed themselves and their baby nutritious food, move for health and pleasure, and tune in, listen, and trust in the innate wisdom of their body and baby. Particularly, one should avoid stress and worry, because these things do negatively impact health. Instead, spend the precious time of pregnancy in awe, wonder, and gratitude. Appreciate the miracle of the human body. How amazing it is that it can make this perfect little being grow inside them.

Our bodies are an expression of our ancestors—that long line of people who have contributed to who we are. As we move into parenthood we are adding a link to that chain. Imagine how powerful it would be if we could cultivate love and appreciation for all of our unique bodies, and pass that on to our next generation. We can choose to see the beauty in the diversity of the world, and we can choose to see ourselves as part of that beauty. We can choose to "change how we see, not how we look" (Connie Sobczak).

For more information see:
- *Health at Every Size: The Surprising Truth About Your Weight* by Linda Bacon
- *Embody: Learning to Love Your Unique Body (And Quiet that Critical Voice)* by Connie Sobczak
- *My Plus Size Pregnancy Guide* by Jen McLellan

OPTIMAL FETAL POSITIONING By Lauren LoBue, Bay Area doula: www.laurenlobue.com

Did you know that the way your baby is positioned in your belly can have a tremendous impact on your labor and birth experience?

WHAT IS OPTIMAL FETAL POSITIONING?

Optimal Fetal Positioning refers to everything you, your baby, your care providers and birth support team can do to ensure that your baby is in the best position for birth. The optimal position is the one that ensures the baby is lined up to fit through your pelvis and the birth canal in the most efficient way possible. Though this depends on the type of pelvis you have, for most people the position which is called left occiput anterior (LOA), or right occiput anterior (ROA) is the most optimal for birth. This means that your baby is head-down, facing your back, with her spine along the left side of your belly. In this position, your baby's head is able to press evenly on your cervix to start labor when it is time and to ensure that labor progresses steadily. Babies rotate, shift and mold slowly throughout their journey through the pelvis and into the world. Helping your baby get into the most efficient position helps support her/him in that journey.

THIS IMAGE ILLUSTRATES BABY IN LOA POSITION

DOES IT WORK FOR EVERYONE?

Fortunately, you do not have to worry about whether your baby is LOA or ROA as your baby's birth approaches. Although LOA is considered the 'norm', it is not every baby's optimal position for birth. Your baby may prefer to be *right* occiput anterior (ROA — head-down, with her back along your right side), or even posterior (also called OP, this position means your baby is head-down, facing your front instead of your back). The good news is that utilizing the tricks and tools described here will ensure that your baby is in the best position for *your baby and your body*. These activities help to *optimize* her position, rather than forcing her into any specific position.

It can be useful to have a skilled doula or birth partner who can help you during labor if the baby needs to change her position in order to relieve pain, restart a labor that has slowed down, or ease back labor. Some of the signs of malposition you may experience before labor begins include back pain, sharp pain at the front of your pelvis (pubic symphysis), feeling hands and feet at the front of your belly, and premature rupture of membranes with no contractions.

WHY DO WE NEED TO PRACTICE OPTIMAL FETAL POSITIONING?

We see more people with babies presenting in positions that might mean longer, harder labors today than in the past. Perhaps the way we use our bodies today may have something to do with this. Earlier societies walked, stood, and squatted more than we do currently in the US. There are still places in the world where this is the case! But for people giving birth in the US, there are many reasons why being mindful of your baby's position is important:

- We spend a lot of time sitting (in the car, on public transit, in the office, at home). Frequent sitting in non- ergonomic seats can cause ligaments and muscles to be tighter than they should be in some areas and looser than they should be in others. This can constrict the amount of space the baby has to maneuver into an optimal position. Most notable among these is the Psoas muscle

- We don't always carry ourselves upright, using good posture.

- Stress and being in chronic fight-or-flight can cause our muscles to be tighter than they were meant to be.

- Many of us have been injured in car accidents, falls, etc. that result in pelvic subluxation (being out of alignment).

WHAT CAN I DO TO PRACTICE OPTIMAL POSTURE AND ALIGNMENT?

Below are some suggestions for ensuring that you have good alignment and posture and that your baby is encouraged to be in her ideal position in your belly. Please keep in mind that each of our bodies is unique, and if any of these suggestions feel uncomfortable or cause pain, *do not do them*. These are only suggestions, and like many suggestions offered to pregnant people, please take what you want and leave the rest. After about 28 weeks, your baby begins to get big enough that practicing these things regularly can impact her position in your belly. Another benefit to practicing these techniques is less low back pain in pregnancy.
It definitely won't hurt to start them whenever, and you don't have to feel bad if you aren't able to stay on top of them as regularly as you'd like. Every little bit helps!

- **Maintain an upright posture** as often as possible and **avoiding slouching, reclining, and leaning back**. Keep the focus on ensuring your **hips are above your knees** when you sit. Use lots of pillows and bolsters behind your back and under your bottom where you sit to help you be comfortable and relaxed in an upright position. Build "nests" made of pillows in your area on the couch so you can relax there at the end of the day.

- Make an effort to **sit on top of your sitz bones** (literally, the bones you feel under you when you sit), which creates a more upright posture naturally. If you're not sure where those bones are, try rocking back and forth while sitting and feel the bones underneath you. When upright and sitting on your sitz bones, your back gets straighter and your pelvis tilts forward, the baby's face likes to be flat against your sacrum, which is the anterior position. When sitting more on your bottom, you assume a slouched position and your pelvis tilts back, which can lend itself to posterior positioning of the baby's head.

- **Consider purchasing a "wedge" seat for the car** to bring your hips and knees level (the cut-out section at the back takes the pressure off of your sacrum and coccyx bone)

- The cat (1) and cow (2) series of yoga poses whenever you feel like it throughout the day. Even 2 or 3 minutes can be effective and feel great.

- Find a **chiropractor** that has experience working with pregnant people and who can help align your pelvis, and release the psoas and tight ligaments.

- Find a **massage therapist** that is skilled in working with pregnant people and especially with Psoas muscle release.

- Consider getting **acupuncture**, for stress and pain relief, which impacts the position of your baby.

- Go to **prenatal yoga classes** that emphasize position in the practice.

The drawing above demonstrates a technique for shifting the baby's position during labor.

HOW CAN A DOULA TRAINED IN OPTIMAL FETAL POSITIONING HELP ME IN MY BIRTH?

A doula can suggest various positions and poses during labor that can help your baby as he shifts and molds through your pelvis. Depending on where you're feeling pain (lower back, frontal pubic area, etc.) your doula can suggest getting into different positions through a few contractions to make it easier for your baby to move. Doulas use sheets, pillows, chairs, bolsters, stools, birth balls, and their own bodies to help you get into these positions and hold them for a while.

WHAT IF I'VE TRIED EVERYTHING AND MY BABY STILL WON'T TURN?

If you've practiced optimizing your baby's position and he won't get into left, or even right, occiput anterior, that's OK! Even if your baby is breech, there can be valid reasons that a baby prefers to be in a certain position — perhaps your specific bodily anatomy encourages him to remain just where he is. Perhaps there's a reason you don't yet know that your baby prefers a certain position. You may find out after his birth, or you may never know. The important thing to remember is that if your baby is in a position during labor that causes you pain, there are some clear signs that a skilled doula or birth partner can see and they may be able to troubleshoot positional problems in the moment.

It's important to trust your baby and your body. You are the best person to birth your baby, and your baby was made for your body. You and your baby are not passive observers; you are active participants and partners in this process.

USING THE SENSE OF SMELL IN LABOR AND BIRTH

SIMPLE AROMATHERAPY RECOMMENDATIONS

First, it is important to understand that using aromatherapy in labor can be a very potent tool; it is to be used in small quantities. Sometimes aromatherapy is not the best tool, as it can be as effective as pharmaceutical drugs and is sometimes counter-indicated with certain medications. For example, using lavender for relaxation in labor can be very soothing, but one of its side effects is a decrease in blood pressure. If you already have low blood pressure, or have an epidural, lavender can cause a dangerous drop in blood pressure and should not be used.

Your sense of smell in labor will be greatly heightened. You may find yourself much more sensitive to smells than you are used to. When using scents and aromatherapies in labor, try taking a short whiff instead of using diffusers, scented candles, or incense sticks. If you find that a scent is too strong, it may give you headaches or make you nauseous. Also, make sure that the people who attend your birth know to stay away from wearing perfumes and scented lotions or shampoos, as these odors can be quite stimulating when you're in labor.

USING ESSENTIAL OILS IN LABOR

Make sure to get 100% essential oil when purchasing these scents, as they are only useful if they are made from a true plant source. Open the bottle and put under the nose, just taking a short breath in. Do not use a diffuser or take internally (in the mouth). Also, check with your birth attendants to make sure that they are not sensitive to these scents before using them.

SCENTS THAT ARE BENEFICIAL

Grapefruit: Essential oil of grapefruit is a very potent energizer. Use this scent in the moments when you feel exhausted or simply need an energy or mood boost. (Partners and birth attendants can also benefit from the use of grapefruit essential oil when labors are long and they need a boost.) Another great effect of smelling grapefruit oil is a reduction in nausea and vomiting, so keep this on hand if you find yourself feeling queasy or if you have a hard time keeping food down.

Peppermint: Essential oil of peppermint is very useful for nausea and vomiting. It also will help you relax your pelvic floor if you find yourself having trouble urinating during or after birth. Smell a little when sitting on the toilet and try putting a couple drops in the toilet water to let the vapors radiate upward around your bottom.

Lavender: Lavender is a potent relaxant to be used whenever you need to decrease anxiety or stress. **Remember: it is not to be used with an epidural or history of low blood pressure.**

Aromatic substances are used as an aid for meditation, altering the mood and eliciting positive memories. Scent can transport our psyches to another time and place or help us focus on the here and now. During pregnancy and birth, the sense of smell is extremely heightened, which allows for full advantage of scent directed relaxation. By practicing this meditation during pregnancy, you will activate wonderful memories, relaxation, and feelings of being safe and loved, which will enhance your happy pregnancy and laboring hormones. *Please note that during labor all scents have the potential to be too stimulating, and even trigger nausea. If you plan to use aromatherapy for relaxation in labor, please see our handout on best practices (page 38).*

List your favorite scents here:

_____
_____
_____
_____

CIRCLE WHICH FEELINGS SCENTS ELICIT WITHIN YOU:

Safe

Love/d

Hug

Open

Laughter

Dancing

Relaxation

Energized

Centered

Acceptance

Ready to work hard and reap rewards!

MY FAVORITE MEMORY AND ITS SCENT:

What essential oils would you like to have for your labor?

SCENT/SMELL RELAXATION

> Anas said, "I never touched silk or velvet softer than the hand of Allah's Messenger (peace be upon him) and never smelled musk or perfumed smoke more pleasant than the smell of Allah's Messenger (peace be upon him)." (Sahih Al-Bukhari)
>
> The messenger of Allah (peace be upon him) said: "Beloved to me in this world of yours is women and scent, and my delight is in prayer." (Nisa'i)

Choose a scent that has qualities that you need right now.
Put the scent close to you so that you can smell it, but don't need to be holding it. You can use an essential oil diffuser, scented candle, incense, or simply put a container with a scent nearby. ***Make sure it is not so strong that it will bother you during the relaxation.*
Get absolutely comfortable in either a sitting or lying position, being supported completely by pillows. Turn off the ringer on your phone and make sure that you are not hungry, thirsty, or needing to use the restroom so that you can be free to fall into a deep relaxing state with no interruptions. It is good to be in a state of wudu. *If you plan to use aromatherapy in labor, please see our handout on best practices on page 38.*

The Practice:

Bismillah.
Take a moment to center your heart on Allah*. Take deep diaphragmatic (belly) breaths, expanding the centering feelings that you have in your heart with every breath. Breathe in through the nose, feeling your belly rise. Breathe out, emptying all the air in your lungs by pulling your bellybutton toward your spine. The speed of your breathing is slow, relaxed, natural and comfortable.

With each out breath release tension in your body. Surrender, and sink into the pillows or wherever you lie.

- Take a deep breath in, breathe out and release your head, neck and, shoulders.

- Take a deep breath in, breathe out and release your chest, mid back, torso and belly.

- Take a deep breath in, breathe out and release your legs, hips, ankles, and feet.

Now turn your attention to the scent and allow yourself to fully experience it: Notice everything: your body, your thoughts, your memories. Let your mind and body be fully in the experience of this wonderful aroma and all it has to offer you. Stay with the scent and this feeling of relaxation as an integrated experience. Let your thoughts just float by** while you breathe and enjoy for as long as is comfortable.

Footnotes for Scent/Smell Relaxation:

The following suggestions pertain to all of the relaxations in this workbook

*Center your heart on Allah: Use whatever means best achieves this goal. Try the following: say salawat (send peace upon The Prophet) , think about The Prophet (peace be upon him), think about Allah, say "Bismillah", "Allah", "Ya Rahman" (Oh Most Gracious) , "Ya Raheem" (Oh Most Merciful), God, the Supreme Being, HU or any other name you have for the sacred originator of all things. If you are not feeling connecting through any of these, try to center yourself with your favorite feeling. If this also isn't effective try to, as a first step, to visualize your favorite memory. If none of these centers you simply focus on your breathing.

** Let your thoughts just float by: if you're having difficulty staying with this experience, try to do a few salawat (sending peace upon The Prophet) and deep breaths. If demanding thoughts keep coming back don't fight them, let them pass and come back to salawat and to feel centered in your chest. Remember, the more you do this the better you will get at it.

As with any pre-written visualizations, we encourage you to replace any language or word use that doesn't flow easily for you; replacing with your own version.

Daily prayer times are the perfect opportunity to enjoy the benefits of relaxation techniques. By taking deeper breaths and tapping into the feelings of calm and centering that are being enhanced, your prayers will serve more readily as a connection to Allah, and a rest for the soul inshaAllah. Everything in Islam is based on our connection to Allah. The word Salat (prayer) means connection.

THE CORNERSTONE METHOD OF CHILDBIRTH EDUCATION

ENGAGE. INFORM. EMPOWER.

CLASS TWO

SENSE: BREATH

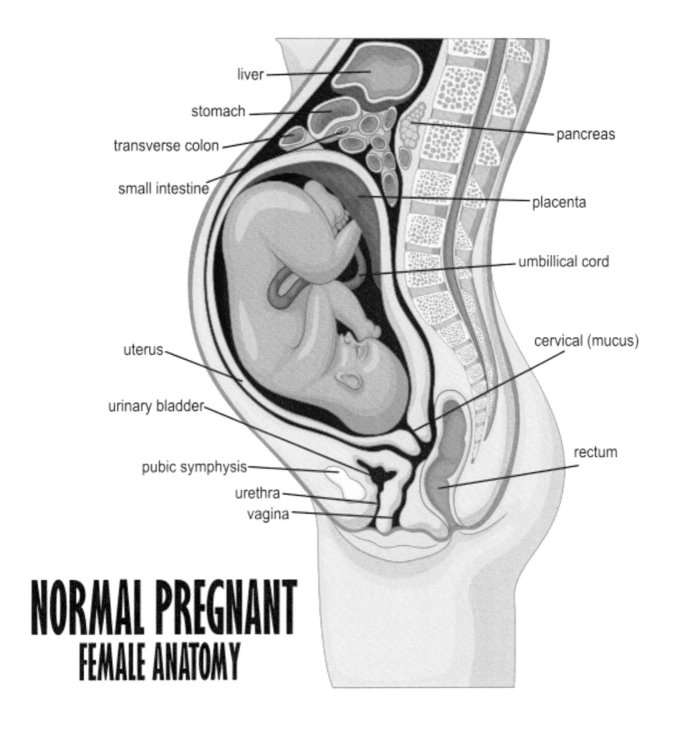

liver

stomach

transverse colon

small intestine

pancreas

placenta

umbillical cord

uterus

cervical (mucus)

urinary bladder

pubic symphysis

urethra

vagina

rectum

NORMAL PREGNANT FEMALE ANATOMY

CERVICAL AND PELVIC CHANGES IN LABOR

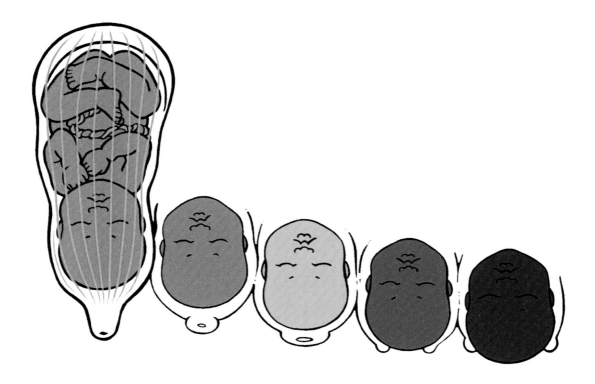

As shown in this illustration, the cervix shortens, thins, and opens during labor.

A WORD ABOUT PROGRESS IN LABOR

There are five things that can be measured in a vaginal exam: Cervical softening (ripening), effacement, dilation, pelvic station, and the baby's position. These are not the only changes that are happening to your body and your baby during labor. Other changes that are considered progress in labor are: the baby's lungs getting ready for breathing, the baby's immune system preparing for extra uterine life, the baby's head molding and birthing person's pelvis stretching to make the baby's journey through the pelvic bones easier, and the breasts getting ready for the first feeding. Though we can get some information about your labor's progress with a vaginal exam, we cannot see or feel everything.

EFFACEMENT AND RIPENING

Ripening is the softening of the cervical tissue that allows it to stretch and open. Effacement is the thinning of the cervix before and during labor. Your cervix will start out about 3-4 centimeters long, thick, and firm. It will shorten completely and become paper-thin during labor - this is called 100% effaced. Some effacement may happen in the days leading up to labor, but for most, the majority of effacement is done during first stage labor. Effacement is measured in percentage (0-100%) during a vaginal exam.

DILATION

Dilation is the opening of the cervix before and during labor.
Your cervix will open to 10 centimeters (also known as "complete") to allow the baby to pass through the uterus.   Some dilation may happen in the weeks leading up to labor, but the majority of dilation happens in first stage labor.   Dilation is measured in centimeters (0-10cm) during a vaginal exam.

PELVIC STATION

Station is the location of the baby's head in relation to the landmarks of your pelvis. Your baby descends during the first and second stage of labor and his movement can be measured in centimeters above or below the spines of your pelvis during a vaginal exam. (+ or − 0-4cm)

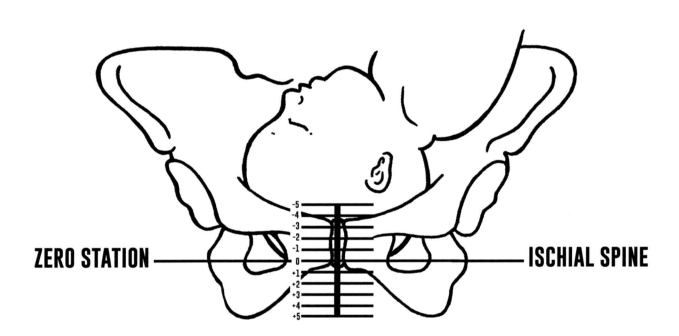

ZERO STATION ———————————————— ISCHIAL SPINE

UTERINE CONTRACTIONS

The uterus has two different muscle fiber types. During contractions, the long muscle fibers run from the top of the uterus to the bottom and pull upward toward the fundus (top of the uterus) to shorten and open the cervix. The round muscle fibers that circle the bottom of the uterus relax as the long muscle fibers pull upward. **These muscle fibers must work coordinately for uterine contractions to be tolerable and efficient in opening the cervix.** Exhaustion, hunger, fear and dehydration can make these fibers work discordantly, which causes painful contractions that do not change the cervix. This is one of many reasons why it is so important to stay fed, hydrated, and rested as much as possible during labor. When contractions are coordinate and progressive, they will continue becoming longer, stronger, and closer together until the birth of your baby. The hormone oxytocin, which is stored and secreted in the posterior pituitary, binds to receptors on the uterus causing it to contract. This process works via positive feedback; the more contractions you have, the more oxytocin your pituitary releases. Oxytocin doesn't just cause uterine contractions; it also facilitates bonding and attachment and puts you into an altered state of consciousness. Therefore, the more coordinate contractions you have, the more opportunity for going into "labor land" - the altered state of consciousness - you get.

WHERE CONTRACTIONS ARE FELT

Most women/laboring people report feeling cramping, tightening, and pressure in a few key areas of the body: lower belly, cervical area, hips, and lower back. Some people will feel their contractions in other places, as well: down their legs, etc. Strong contractions, as labor progresses are felt from the lower back, all the way around the full belly.

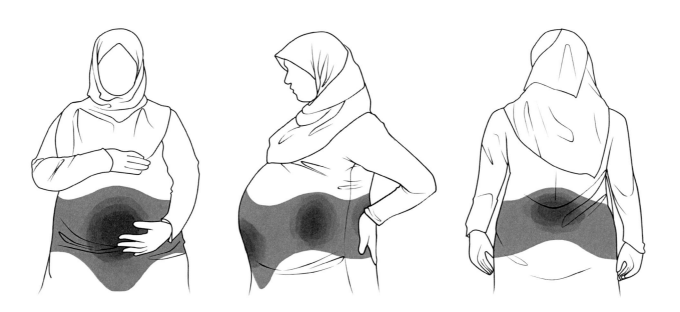

USING THE SENSE OF BREATH IN LABOR

Breathe at your own pace. Your breathing may be slow or fast, but it should always be deep and centered on the belly, and focused on releasing tension on the out breath. You use your breath in labor for oxygenation AND relaxation. Typically, you will find yourself taking deep breaths at the beginning of your contractions, as your body knows that your baby needs a store of oxygen to get through the coming contraction. Breathe steadily throughout the contraction, focusing your energy downward. It is helpful to take a nice, deep, cleansing breath at the end of the contraction to bring oxygen back to you and baby, as well as to let go of any tension from the contraction that just ended

**Partners, if she/he/they start to breathe from her chest and/or shallowly, gently remind her/them/he to come back to deep breaths and to re-focus her energy on relaxation.

- Remind her/him/them to relax key tension points whenever breathing out by showing and touching – use non-verbal labor support.

- Notice where the breath is focused – it should be lower in the body, not in the chest.

- Notice the sounds being made when breathing. Are they guttural and low or high pitched and shrill? *You may need to remind her over and over again to bring her energy downward.*

- If she/he/they get nauseous in labor, it may be from energy being stuck in chest. If you can help them bring their energy and breath down to the belly, the nausea will pass.

Labor will take you to hills, valleys, mountaintops, and raging rivers. Your breathing will adjust itself to the appropriate rate, speed, and depth of inspiration based on oxygen requirements during these different experiences. The journey through labor will bring with it intensity of physical effort and sensation, or emotional experiences which you may respond to in fast, rapid, shallow breaths. Sometimes this is necessary for getting through an intense moment. **This type of breathing is not beneficial to the laboring person or the baby if it continues for more than 15-30 seconds,** which is the amount of time it takes to get through those intense peaks. This breathing can also have the negative effect of triggering the flight or fight response, resulting in what we know as the tension, fear, pain cycle. Once the flight or flight response is activated, oxygen is redistributed to help the distressed person get away from danger (real or perceived), and less oxygen goes to the organs that are not needed for immediate survival, hence the baby gets less oxygen.

GROUP BREATHING EXERCISE

Breathe deeply, in through the nose and out through the mouth. As you breathe **in,** your belly should **rise** and as you breathe out, your belly should **fall.** ** You can imagine filling your belly with air as you breathe in and pulling your belly button toward your spine as you breathe out.

PATTERNED BREATHING (hee, hee, hoo)
List physical and emotional responses:

DEEP BELLY/DIAPHRAGMATIC BREATHING
List physical and emotional responses:

EVEN DEEPER BELLY/DIAPHRAGMATIC BREATHING GUIDED BY YOUR COURSE LEADER
List physical and emotional responses:

BREATH RELAXATION

To the righteous soul it will be said: "O fully satisfied soul!
Return to your Lord, well pleased with Him and well-pleasing to Him.".
(Surah Al-Fajr (#89), Ayaat 27-28)

Allah said to the angels during the creation of Adam (peace be upon him): "when I complete his moulding and breath into him of My spirit, kneel down and prostrate before him." (Surah Al-Hijr (#15), Ayah 29)

Get absolutely comfortable in either a sitting or lying position, being supported completely by pillows. Turn off the ringer on your phone and make sure that you are not hungry, thirsty, or needing to use the restroom so that you can be free to fall into a deep relaxing state with no interruptions. It is good to be in a state of wudu. It is ok if you fall asleep. You need as much rest as you can get; consider it a bonus if you get to catch a nap!

Have a partner or friend read this script to you. As they read, have them pause for a minute in between each statement. When the reader gets to the end of the script, they can quietly sneak out and leave you to continue your relaxation until you are ready to come out of it. If you would prefer to do this practice on your own, simply record yourself reading the script and play it back once you are nice and comfortable.

The Practice:

Bismillah.
Take a moment to center your heart on Allah*. Take deep diaphragmatic (belly) breaths, expanding the centering feelings that you have in your heart with every breath. Breathe in through your nose, feeling your belly rise. Breathe out slowly, emptying all of the air in your lungs by pulling your bellybutton toward your spine. The speed of your breathing is slow, relaxed, natural and comfortable. With each breath out, release tension in your body, surrender, and sink deeper into the pillows or where you lie.

- Take a deep breath in, breathe out and release your head, neck, shoulders, arms, and hands.

- Take a deep breath in, breathe out and release your chest, mid back, torso and belly.

- Take a deep breath in, breathe out and release your legs, hips, ankles and feet.

Close your eyes.
Imagine you are at the seaside. It is beautiful and the waves are coming and going in a natural rhythm. The sea air smells wonderful. You are surrounded by Allah's mercy. You breath it in, deeply refreshed and calm. The wind, the sands, the sea are all in harmony to the rhythm of the

waves. Allah's mercy is manifest in everything. You are warmed by the sun and the gentle breezes brush your cheeks.

You instinctively want to take long deep breaths of the lovely sea air into your lungs. The misty air fills your lungs and circulates through your body, oxygenating all of your cells.

You find that in order to get a fulfilling breath, you must breath from your diaphragm. You feel your lungs, and belly expand with each breath in, being filled with Allah's mercy. Breathing out feels just as good. You feel that your cells are being cleansed as you deeply release and let go of the used up air and of unwanted feelings.

Breathe in and oxygenate you and your baby, breathe out and release anywhere that there is tension in your body. (say this three times)

Stay at the ocean as long as you are comfortable.

THE CORNERSTONE METHOD OF CHILDBIRTH EDUCATION

ENGAGE. INFORM. EMPOWER.

CLASS THREE

SENSE: BODY AWARENESS

STAGES OF LABOR

There are three stages of labor: First stage, second stage, and third stage. In first stage labor, full cervical effacement and dilation is achieved.
This first stage is broken into three phases: Early labor, active labor, and transition. Second stage labor is the pushing phase, when the baby is born and third stage is the birth of the placenta.

The end of pregnancy will bring many new sensations, as your body is getting ready to go into labor. Though these signs cannot tell you exactly when your labor will begin, they are good indicators that it is coming sometime soon.

PRELABOR SYMPTOMS

- Sporadic backaches and period like cramps

- Braxton hicks contractions

- Loss of the mucus plug

- Bloody show

- Irritability and mood swings

- Lightening (the baby "drops")

- Nesting instinct

- Nausea

- Loose bowels

- Rounds of contractions

WHAT IS A "ROUND OF CONTRACTIONS?"

First: there is **no such thing as false labor**.
Your body will sometimes need to try a few "practice runs" before labor fully takes off. Practice labor (or labor "rounds") is defined as contractions that start at 5 minutes apart, lasting about a minute long, and are strong enough that you have to stop and breathe with them. Practice labor contractions **do not** get longer, stronger, or closer together. These contractions will typically begin between 11pm and 3 am and go away until the next night, or they may start again on another day. This practice is not only O.K, it is actually good!

WHAT IS HAPPENING

- Long muscles and short round muscles of the uterus are learning to co-ordinate.

- Uterus toning

- Cervical softening

- Cervical effacement

- Baby is adjusting their position, molding, and dropping into the pelvis.

If you can embrace practice labor as a positive part of your pregnancy and birth and take naps to stay caught up on your sleep, you will find that you may go into labor with a very ripe (soft), effaced, and partially dilated cervix. You will also be well rested and ready to meet the challenge of your labor. We guarantee that your labor will be shorter than it would have been without all that wonderful preparation! What cannot be known until the exact moment that your baby is born is how long your labor will be. Remember: plan on 24-36 hours total for a first baby!

IS IT A ROUND OF CONTRACTIONS?

Here's how to find out:

- Eat a little

- Drink a little

- Change activity – go for a short walk or lie down to rest

- Take a bath

If you do all of these things and contractions continue, it most likely is not a round and your labor will progress further.

FIRST STAGE LABOR

During this stage your cervix will fully efface and dilate. Typically, first time laborers will experience a long first stage. Everyone is different, but expect to be in this stage for at least 24-36 hours if this is your first time. Second time labors typically move faster, sometimes lasting as little as 1-3 hours once active labor begins. This stage is divided into three phases: Early labor, active labor, and transition. If you have a doula, they will be joining you a little later in first stage, typically in active labor. Though you can usually tell how labor is progressing by timing contractions, the emotional signs will let you know what phase you are in. It's not all about the numbers. You will need to put every piece of the puzzle together to determine what phase of first stage labor is happening and when going to the hospital is best for you. If you plan to take pain medication, it is recommended to wait until 5 centimeters dilation for an epidural, and opiate medications should be given earlier.

EARLY LABOR SIGNS AND SYMPTOMS

Emotional signpost: **Excitemen**t

- Typically, laboring people experience this phase for 12-24 hours, but some laboring people do not even have early labor.
- Contractions tend to be sporadic and about 5-30 minutes apart and 30-45 seconds in duration.

- Contractions will be mild and not too strong to take your full focus.

- You can still walk and talk through these contractions.

- You will still feel comfortable being fully clothed, and hungry.

- Typically, the cervix dilates to 3cm in this phase.

TO DO:

- Eat

- Drink

- Relax

- Rest

- Short walks – nothing too strenuous

- Cuddle and kiss

- Funny movies

NOTES:

Early labor is a time to enjoy one another and save energy for the work that lies ahead. Take time to connect and feel good in early labor.   This will boost oxytocin production and will get your labor off to a good start. Baby will really enjoy feeling the love and relaxation and so will you.

In early labor, we recommend snuggling and kissing to help aide oxytocin production and promote feelings of well being, connection, and love.

ACTIVE LABOR SIGNS AND SYMPTOMS

Emotional signpost: **Serious**

- First timers usually experience this phase for 8-14+ hours, but it can vary greatly from person to person.

- Contractions are typically 3-7 minutes apart and no longer sporadic, lasting about a minute in duration or sometimes up to 90 seconds toward the end of this phase.

- Contractions will be stronger, longer, and closer together compared to early labor and will continue to move in this direction.

- You cannot walk or talk through these contractions and will be very focused on your work; turning inward.

- You may start to feel hot or constricted by clothing.

- Many people no longer feel hungry in active labor.

- Typically, the cervix dilates to 7cm in this phase.

TO DO

- Eat

- Drink

- Rest between contractions

- Change positions and empty bladder every 1 ½ hours

FOR LABOR SUPPORT/PARTNERS

- Try to create a dark, safe space. A laboring person's three basic needs are **quiet, privacy, and darkness.**

- If you must ask questions, make sure they are easy to answer and are asked in between contractions.

- Give bites of food and sips of fluid in between contractions.

- Give active labor management when needed; not everyone needs hands on support.

- Limit observers

- Use non verbal communication for relaxation reminders, paying attention to key points (jaw, face, hands, shoulders, hips)

Continue to connect physically and emotionally through active labor, enhancing the pain relieving hormones endorphin and oxytocin. When a laboring person feels supported, held, and safe they will allow themselves to go to a deeper place of surrender.

Sometimes touch is too intense once labor gets active. Simply holding hands can be a very effective tool for labor support in this (and any) active phase.

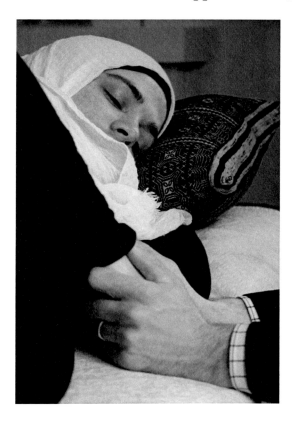

TRANSITION SIGNS AND SYMPTOMS

Emotional signpost: **Self-doubt/Feeling like you cannot go on.**

- This is the shortest and most difficult phase of first stage labor.
- First timers typically experience this phase from 3 contractions to 3 hours. The typical length is 45 minutes.
- Contractions are typically 1-3 minutes apart and have multiple peaks.
- The contractions are both opening the cervix and pushing the baby down.
- Shaking
- Sweating
- Vomiting
- Burping
- Extreme hot and cold flashes
- bloody show (from cervix changing rapidly to fully dilated)
- Usually the laboring person says that they cannot go on or continue at this point.
- The end of transition will be full cervical dilation.

TO DO

- Trust your body

- Know that you are safe

- Surrender to the intensity

- Accept support from caregivers, partner, and family.

NOTES:

If you get scared during transition, remember that everything you are feeling is your own body's power. Your body is incredibly strong and will not give you anything that you cannot handle in a normal birth. Surrender to your body and let yourself give in to the power of your labor.

FOR LABOR SUPPORT/PARTNERS

- Give active labor support continuously through this phase if needed.

- Three contractions using a technique, then try something else. Keep rotating techniques.

- Strong verbal encouragement

- Take charge routine if needed: Firm hold on the shoulders, eye-to-eye contact, and coaching through each contraction.

- Remind her/him/them that she/he/they are safe and that this is normal.

Strong face-to-face support is sometimes needed in transition to get through each contraction. Anchor her by firmly holding on to her arms or shoulders, stay close, and connected creating a sense of safety and a space that is held for her to completely surrender to this transition.

PAIN IN LABOR

While you can expect to feel intensity and strong sensations in labor, not everyone experiences pain. The sensations of contractions will be intense and transformative, but they don't always hurt. Contractions build in intensity, peak, then release and end. You will have breaks in between contractions that will give you time to rest and gather your strength for the next one.

Relaxation is the best remedy for pain in labor. While your uterus is doing the hard work of contracting, your only job is to keep your body completely relaxed so that you have energy throughout the labor and birth. Furthermore, the more relaxed you get, the stronger your pain relieving hormones will feel.

REMEMBER

Fear causes tension and tension causes pain. When you can go into your labor relaxed and trusting in your body and baby, you will have the opportunity to have an enjoyable, empowering, and even blissful birth.

Loving touch, along with a comfortable environment exponentially increases a relaxed state and your pain relieving hormones. Allow your partner(s) or birth team to fully support you. Trust in your body, your baby, and your birth. Say yes to your contractions and surrender to the intensity of your body; enjoy all that your body is and can do. You are capable, strong, powerful, and supported.

TIMING CONTRACTIONS

Partners: It is not necessary to time every single contraction. This practice is used to determine the swiftness of labor. Every time you notice that labor has picked up, time a few contractions to see how they are different from the previous pattern. Labor contractions when progressing will continue to become longer, stronger, and closer together. If you are noticing that the contractions are doing this very quickly, then it's likely the labor is moving more swiftly.

INFORMATION TO TAKE NOTE OF

- Contraction length: How long is the contraction lasting from beginning to end?

- Contraction frequency: How far apart are the contractions? To determine frequency, you must time from **the beginning of one contraction to the beginning of the next.**

There are many phone apps that will help time contractions and will tell you the length and frequency. If you are doing it the old fashioned way and using a watch, make sure you count the seconds as well as the minutes. We recommend using a watch with a backlight so that you can time contractions in the dark.

QUIZ

- Contraction begins at 4:45:30

- Contraction ends at 4:46:45

- Contraction begins at 4:48:30

- Contraction ends at 4:49:45

- Contraction begins at 4:51:30

- Contraction ends at 4:52:45

1. How many contractions did you count? _____

2. How long are they lasting? _____

3. How far apart are they? _____

BODY AWARENESS RELAXATION

> I went to the Messenger of Allah (peace be upon him) and he asked me, "Have you come to inquire about piety?" I replied in the affirmative. Then he said, "Ask your heart regarding it. Piety is that which contents the soul and comforts the heart, and sin is that which causes doubts and perturbs the heart, even if people pronounce it lawful and give you verdicts on such matters again and again."   (Ahmad and Ad-Darmi).

> All that is in the heavens and the earth glorifies Allah, and He is the All-Mighty, the All-Wise. (Surah Al-Hadid (@57), Ayah 1)

Through tensing and then relaxing each part of the body, you will identify areas that hold the most tension and learn how to efficiently release them. In labor, holding tension and gripping or tightening any muscle group can have a negative effect of prompting the fear, tension, pain cycle. The most common areas that tension is held in labor are the jaw, shoulders, hands, abdomen, hips, and buttocks. This tension wastes valuable energy and may prevent labor's progress. Conversely, relaxation of your muscles reduces your heart rate and blood pressure, as well as decreases your respiration rates. Relaxation is also an excellent tool to conserve energy for the duration of your labor. Remember: after first stage labor, you'll still have the pushing phase and will want to be as rested as possible in preparation.

Get absolutely comfortable in either a sitting or lying position, being supported completely by pillows. Turn off the ringer on your phone and make sure that you are not hungry, thirsty, or needing to use the restroom so that you can be free to fall into a deep relaxing state with no interruptions. It is good to be in a state of wudu.

Have a partner or friend read this script to you. As they read, have them pause for a few seconds in between each statement. When the reader gets to the end of the script, they can quietly sneak out and leave you to continue your relaxation until you are ready to come out of it. If you would prefer to do this practice on your own, simply record yourself reading the script and play it back once you are nice and comfortable.

The Practice:

Bismillah.
Take a moment to center your heart on Allah*. Take deep diaphragmatic (belly) breaths, expanding the centering feelings that you have in your heart with every breath. Breathe in through your nose, feeling your belly rise. Breathe out slowly, emptying all of the air in your lungs by pulling your bellybutton toward your spine. The speed of your breathing is slow, relaxed, natural and comfortable. With each breath out, release tension in your body, surrender, and sink deeper into the pillows or where you lie.

- Take a deep breath in, breathe out and release your head, neck, shoulders, arms, and hands.

- Take a deep breath in, breathe out and release your chest, mid back, torso and belly.

65

- Take a deep breath in, breathe out and release your legs, hips, ankles and feet.

During this relaxation I will ask you to tense various muscles throughout your body. Please do this without straining. You do not need to exert yourself, just contract each muscle firmly but gently as you breathe in. If you feel uncomfortable at any time, you can simply relax and breathe normally.

Bring your awareness to your feet and toes. Breathe in deeply through your nose, and as you do, gently flex your feet upward toward your shin. Hold your breath for just a few seconds and then release the muscles in your feet as you breathe out. Feel the tension in your feet wash away as you exhale. Notice how different your feet feel when tensed and when they are relaxed. Feel yourself relaxing more and more deeply with each breath. Your whole body is becoming heavier, softer, and more relaxed as each moment passes.
Draw in a deep breath and tighten your leg muscles. Hold for a few seconds, and then let it all go as you breathe out. Feel your muscles relax, and the tension washing away with your out-breath.

Take another breath and this time and gradually tighten all the muscles in your legs, from your feet to your buttocks. Do this in whatever way feels natural and comfortable to you. Hold it - and now release all these large strong muscles as you breathe out. Enjoy the sensation of release as you become even more deeply relaxed.

Now bring your awareness to your abdomen. Draw in a nice, deep breath tightening these muscles. Imagine you are trying to touch your belly button to your spine. Now release your breath and let all of these abdominal muscles relax. Notice the sensation of relief that comes from letting go. Once again, draw in a deep breath, tightening your abdominal muscles. Hold for a few seconds, and then let them relax completely as you exhale and release all tension.

Now bring your awareness to the muscles in your back. As you slowly breathe in, arch your back slightly and tighten these muscles. Release your breath and let your back muscles relax completely. Again, draw in a deep breath, tightening your back muscles. Hold for the count of three, and then let them relax and release completely.
Now take your attention to your shoulder and neck muscles. As you slowly draw in a nice, deep breath, pull your shoulders up toward your ears tightening them firmly. Breathe out completely and allow the contracted neck and shoulder muscles to go loose and limp, fully relaxed.

Once more, pull your shoulders up toward your ears and tighten their muscles firmly. Let our your breath and feel the tension subside as you relax and breathe out. Feel the heaviness in your body now, enjoying the relaxation. Feel yourself becoming heavier and heavier. Feel yourself becoming more and more deeply relaxed. You are calm, secure, and at peace.

Now it's time to let go of all the tension in your arms and hands. Start with your upper arms. As you breathe in, raise your wrists towards your shoulders and tighten the muscles in your upper arms. Hold that breath and that contraction for just a moment, and then gently lower your arms and breathe all the way out. You may feel a warm, burning sensation in your muscles when you tighten them. Feel how relaxing it is to release that tightness and to breathe away all tension. Your arms are completely limp. As you curl your upper arms again, tighten the muscles as you breathe in. Breathe in deeply. As you breathe out, relax your arms completely, even more than the time before.

Now bring your awareness to your forearms. As you breathe in, curl your hands inwards as though you are trying to touch the inside of your elbows with your fingertips. As you breathe out, feel the tension subside as your forearms relax and release.

Again, take a deep breath in, tightening the muscles in your forearms. Hold it for a moment, and then release. Feel the tension washing away completely. Your arms are fully relaxed.

Take a breath in and tightly clench your fists. When you have finished breathing in, hold for the count of three, and then release your hands. Your hands are so soft and relaxed. Take another deep breath in, clenching your fists. Hold for the count of three and then release your hands once more. Let your fingers go limp. Your arms and hands are feeling so heavy and relaxed. Take a couple of nice long slow breaths now, and just relax completely. Feel yourself slipping even deeper into a state of complete rest.

Tighten the muscles in your face by squeezing your eyes shut and clenching your lips together as you take a deep breath in. Hold it for the count of three, then breathe out and relax all your facial muscles. Feel your face softening completely, your tongue loose in your mouth. Once more, breathe in deeply while you tighten the muscles in your eyes and lips. And release.

Bring your awareness to the muscles in your jaw. Take a deep breath in, opening your mouth as wide as you can. Feel your jaw muscles stretching and tightening as your mouth opens. Exhale and let your jaw go slack, feeling your tongue limp and loose in your mouth. Breathe into your jaw and release any tension that still remains. Again, fill your lungs with air, opening your mouth wide. Breathe out and let your mouth relax completely. Let your breath flow all the way out of your lungs.

You are now completely relaxed from the tips of your toes to the top of your head. Enjoy this feeling and take a few more minutes to rest.

Relax. Listen to the sound of your breathing and enjoy the lovely, warm sensation of full, pure physical relaxation. If you have the time, feel free to fall asleep. You will wake feeling completely rejuvenated, relaxed, and energized.

THE CORNERSTONE METHOD OF CHILDBIRTH EDUCATION

ENGAGE. INFORM. EMPOWER.

CLASS FOUR

SENSE: TOUCH

SECOND STAGE LABOR

This is the pushing stage. The contractions will change to be expulsive, meaning during the peaks of these contractions your uterus will bear down to expel the baby from your body. The contractions will slow down to about 3-5 minutes apart, lasting about 90 seconds, and will have three peaks. Second stage can last for many hours, but most first timers will push for around two. Though there are no official emotional signposts in second stage, most people cycle through the three from first stage labor: excitement, seriousness, and self-doubt. Your baby will be actively participating in the labor process by making many twists and turns to negotiate the bones of your pelvis. Pushing usually feels good if you are working with your body by pushing at the peaks of the contractions and you will most likely feel a strong urge to bear down during these peaks. This bearing down urge is a direct effect of the baby moving down and stimulating stretch receptors in the vagina, which stimulates the release of oxytocin. While the baby moves down, she will slowly stretch the vaginal tissues by advancing towards the opening then going back in. Sometimes this is referred to three steps forward, two steps back. You will feel most of the sensations as baby moves out of your body in the perineum and rectum, and can expect to feel a burning, stretching sensation as he emerges.

TO DO

- Get into a position that allows for engagement of your abdominal muscles.

- Get into a position that feels powerful for you.

- Wait to actively push until you feel the urge to bear down.

- Make sure if you are in a lying position to not flatten your sacrum.

- C-curve to your back

- Use your breath for power

- Change positions frequently to help baby negotiate the bones of the pelvis

- Use upright positions that work with gravity to help baby move down

- Warm compresses on the perineum

- Touch the baby's head as it emerges

- Use a mirror to watch pushing progress

You can see that in the drawing on the left, the woman is sitting directly on her sacrum, reducing the ability of the pelvic outlet to expand. On the right hand photo, she is lifting up her bottom to open the pelvis, creating much more space for the baby. A support person helps by holding her foot in place as she pushes.

THE TRUTH ABOUT SQUATTING

The squat position can be fantastic for second stage, as it works with gravity and opens the pelvic outlet to make more room for baby. This position is only recommended once the baby is engaged and at least at zero station, as it reduces the diameter of the pelvic inlet. ** **We also recommend squatting during active labor and transition if the baby is at zero station or below. Don't worry about timing, follow your bodies cues. Squatting usually will feel good if it is what you and baby need.** **

Most people believe that in an optimal squat the feet are pointed outward, which is not correct. When the feet point outward, the sit bones move closer together and the pelvic outlet diameter is decreased.

In an optimal squat, the feet are pointed straight in front of the body. When your feet are pointed straight in front of you, the sit bones open and the pelvic outlet diameter gets larger, making more space for baby. Most of us are not very comfortable in this position, so it might be necessary to put a pillow or bolster under your heels when you are holding a squat position.

This photo demonstrates how much squatting can change the pelvic outlet diameter:

TIPS FOR LABOR SUPPORT/PARTNERS IN SECOND STAGE

- Keep your partner calm.

- Whisper encouraging words and take an active support role only if needed.

- Hold a leg.

- Cheerlead if needed.

- Cool washcloths to the forehead, neck, and chest.

- Keep a basin close by. A lot of people will vomit in second stage, which helps push the baby down.

PUSHING WITH AN EPIDURAL

- Try waiting until the baby is at least +2 station before actively pushing. This is called "laboring down".

- Consider turning the medication down or off to experience more feeling, which helps you understand how and where to push.

- Consider changing positions frequently if second stage is prolonged.

THIRD STAGE LABOR

Usually within 5-30 minutes post birth, the placenta will be delivered. Immediately after your baby is born, your uterus will start to contract, causing it to shrink. As the uterus shrinks down, the surface area that the placenta is attached to becomes smaller, causing the placenta to detach from the uterine wall. Once the placenta has detached, you can easily push it out without much effort. Remember, your placenta does not have bones and a full baby has just paved the way out. After the placenta is born, your provider will inspect it to make sure that it is intact and will continue on with management of your immediate postpartum period.

THIRD STAGE MANAGEMENT

There are 2 distinctive styles of managing the 3rd stage of labor, otherwise known as the delivery of the placenta.

One style is called "expectant or physiological" management, and the other is called "active" management. In general, expectant management is used more often by out of hospital birth midwives and active management is used more often in the hospital setting.

Expectant management practice supports the physiologic process of the body solely pushing out the placenta without any added help. The midwife feels comfortable waiting for post birth contractions to push the placenta off of the wall of the uterus. If this does not happen within a specific amount of time (usually within the hour, average 20 minutes) or if there is an indication to intervene, the midwife will step in and help. She may help the mother by facilitating an upright position, possibly a squat or using the birth stool to make use of gravity. She may also utilize herbs, homeopathy, or an injection of pitocin (synthetic oxytocin) as she deems appropriate. Active management practitioners believe that stepping in and getting the placenta delivered within 5-15 minutes after the birth of the baby is safer than waiting for the body to expel the placenta on it's own. Active management includes synthetically activating uterine contractions by giving a shot of pitocin right after the baby is born and rubbing the mother's belly to aide in contractions. At the same time, cord traction (pulling on the cord) may be used to help birth the placenta.

We encourage you to research these methods and ask your care providers about their management style. If you don't feel comfortable with the answers that you get, you may want to consider asking who might be available for your birth that is a proponent of the style you feel most comfortable and confident with.

NOTES:

IMMEDIATELY AFTER BIRTH

The physiological process of birth is not complete immediately after the baby is born. There is an important bonding sequence that unfolds for the first hour and a half after birth, starting with the emergence of the baby and ending with the baby and birthing person falling into a restorative and neurologically supportive sleep at the 2 hour post birth mark.

THE SEQUENCE

- The baby is born

- Baby takes his/her first breaths

- Baby goes directly onto their birth parent, skin-to-skin (which can also be accomplished when a fine layer of fabric is between them)

- Baby starts the process of slowly unfolding into the outer world

- A hormonal cascade of oxytocin and epinephrine is helping the baby and her birth parent to be alert and receptive to each other, giving enough energy and lucidity to explore each other, bond, fall in love, and in essence, becoming 'addicted' to one other.

- All senses are heightened: The baby will smell his birth parent's skin, and will open her eyes to search for her parents' faces. *This is when you will want the lights low and no flashes if there are photos being taken.*

- Once she finds her parents faces, she will take her time to gaze at and neurologically imprint them.

- The next step is licking, smelling and rooting for the breast.

- The baby, when left alone can and will step crawl up and self attach to the breast. Sometimes, baby needs a little help getting attached to the breast if there are disturbances in the room or any medications on board.

- This sequential process can take as little as 20 minutes or up to 1 ½ hours. At about the two hour mark, the epinephrine starts to wane, prolactin and oxytocin take over, and the baby falls asleep; sometimes for a few hours.

- Though it is rare to witness this full sequence when birth takes place at the hospital, many hospitals now take pride in allowing skin-to-skin contact for the first 20 minutes to 1 ½ hours post birth. Find out what your hospital's immediate post birth protocols are, and if they do not include waiting for the first two hours to start their newborn exam and interventions, you can add it as a request to your birth plan. If everything is normal with you and baby, listening to the baby's heart and lungs and taking his temperature can be done without baby being taken to the warming table. These assessments can all be done when baby is skin-to-skin on your body. Your body temperature will regulate the baby's and they will be much more calm and alert if not separated from you.

- If the person who gave birth is not able to have skin-to-skin contact with baby immediately after the birth, the baby can be on the partner.

NOTES:

WHAT MAKES YOU FEEL SAFE?

Starting to think of ways to create a safe space for your birth.

Who do I feel safe and comfortable around?

_____

Who do I turn to when I am under stress?

_____

What sounds soothe me?

_____
_____
_____
_____

Songs that I would like to add to my birth playlist:

_____
_____
_____
_____

Affirmations that make me feel strong:

_____
_____
_____
_____

Any items that I like to have near when I am stressed or scared:

CHOOSING YOUR BIRTH TEAM

Birth is not a spectator sport! Everyone who attends has a job to do. Some suggestions of criteria when choosing who will attend your birth:

☐ They are comfortable being around your nudity during and after the birth

☐ You will be comfortable being nude around them

☐ They are comfortable with your chosen birth plan and environment

☐ They are comfortable with your forms of religious expression

☐ They will not get scared when labor gets intense

☐ You will not be stressed around them when the labor gets intense

☐ You can let go and get "primal" in front of them

☐ They will not be offended if you ask them to leave the room at any time in the labor and birth

☐ You will feel comfortable asking them to leave the room at any time in the labor and birth

☐ They get along with your partner

☐ They get along with everyone in your birth support team

If you are left with unchecked boxes, you may want to have a conversation about these topics with your birth support team before making any decisions to invite them to attend. **We are mammals and we labor as mammals do.** When cats birth their kittens, they will typically find a space that is dark, quiet, and private before giving birth to their young. They will even stop their labors mid-birth if they feel like they are being observed or are in any danger. We humans go through this same process; we have the same hormonal mechanisms. If we do not feel totally safe in our birth environment or feel like we are being judged or observed, the flight or fight response takes over and our bodies release stress hormones (catecholamines) that will slow contractions down or cause them to be unusually painful. **Your birth outcome's success depends on your trust in the people who are there to help, as well as your comfort in your birth environment.** This is your experience and your feelings of comfort and safety are the most important thing to consider when choosing where and with whom you give birth.

CHOOSING YOUR BIRTH LOCATION

Did you know that couples in the US tend to spend more time researching the car they are going to buy than their birth location or chosen care providers? Something to take into consideration when making this very important decision is that the outcome of your birth experience will affect you, the baby, and your family for the rest of your lives. Birth is a right of passage; a nuanced process that takes you to the edge of what you know about yourself and your capabilities, leaving you completely transformed. Birth is also incredibly beneficial for the baby. It prepares her for extra uterine life by preparing her lungs for breathing air and activating her immune system. Vaginal birth also benefits the baby by colonizing his gut with good bacteria from his mother, preparing his digestive system for lifelong healthy function. Juli Tilsner: midwife and educator says, "The outcome of your birth will be directly impacted by the belief systems of those you choose to assist with your pregnancy and delivery." Who you surround yourself with, negative or positive stories you hear about pregnancy and birth, and the story that you have heard your whole life about your own birth all affect your expectations and perceptions about what and how your birth can be. You are absolutely affected by the perspectives of the books you read, shows you watch, the practitioner you hire, friends and family, and your doula. Consider that you are putting time and energy into the outcome of your birth by practicing The Cornerstone Method. To get the outcome you are working toward, you also will need to choose a provider and place to birth that you trust.

QUESTIONS TO ASK YOURSELF ABOUT YOUR BIRTH LOCATION AND TEAM

- Do I feel autonomous?

- Do I feel heard?

- Am I treated with respect?

- Am I given true informed choice?

- Is my care collaborative or hierarchical?

- Do I feel comfortable asking questions?

- When I ask questions, am I satisfied with the way they are answered?

QUESTIONS TO ASK YOURSELF ABOUT THE INFORMATION YOU ARE GIVEN ABOUT LABOR AND BIRTH

- Are the books I read from a positive birth perspective?

- Do the books I read make me feel empowered?

- Are the books I read long lists of things that might possibly go wrong during birth?

- Do I see positive natural births in the media?

- Do the shows I watch about birth excite me?

- Do the shows I watch about birth scare me?

- When my family, friends, and co-workers tell me their birth stories, do I leave feeling positive about my own experience and body.

- When my family, friends, and co-workers tell me their birth stories, do I leave feeling fearful and less trusting about my own experience and body?

When you are satisfied with your care providers and are partners in the decision making process during your pregnancy and birth, you will be left with an empowered and satisfying birth story/experience, no matter what the outcome is. **We want you to remember: it is never too late to switch providers. You can transfer your care even on the last day of your pregnancy. If you do not like the care you are receiving and are still pregnant, consider finding another provider or location.**

BIRTH LOCATION AND PROVIDER OPTIONS

HOME

Home birth, under the care of a midwife is an option for low risk, healthy pregnant people. The **Midwifery Model of Care** includes: "Monitoring the physical, psychological, and social well-being of the mother throughout the childbearing cycle. Providing the mother with individualized education, counseling, and prenatal care, continuous hands-on assistance during labor and delivery, and postpartum support." - http://mana.org/about-midwives/midwifery-model

The midwifery model is also fully inclusive as a "family centered event". Siblings that witness the birth are known to bond more and have less rivalry, as they are being fully included in the birth process.

Each state has its own legal status for midwifery practice. Nurse-Midwives practice legally in all 50 U.S. states, including The District of Columbia, and Certified Professional Midwives are legally authorized to practice in 28 states. Certified Nurse Midwives (CNM) are nurses that have become midwives through a hospital based training. Certified Professional Midwives (CPM) have gotten their certification through a Midwifery College or a Midwifery Institute program, which are 3 year programs that have stringent academic and hands-on skills requirements that are attained through training, education and supervised clinical experiences in out of hospital based settings followed by successful completion of a written examination. CPMs must pass a board-certifying exam, called the NARM - *North American Registry of Midwives*. States such as California require CPMs to become licensed, and this licensure is based on the same NARM exam. Whichever title your midwife has, be assured she/he/they will bring the same standard of care throughout your time together and will have **adequate medical equipment to safely deliver your baby at home**. Typically, there is very little need for intervention at a home birth. If there is an issue that arises in labor, you and your midwife will have a plan in place to move your labor and birth to a hospital for extra support and safety. Because midwives want the best possible outcome for you and your baby, they are very careful to monitor both you and baby to determine well being and will transfer to the hospital if necessary in a timely manner. For this reason, emergencies at home are rare. If there is a true emergency, midwives are trained to deal with them and have the equipment to attend and stabilize until you and/or baby get the additional medical help that you need.

FREESTANDING BIRTH CENTER

These are essentially home births at a center that is not your home.
You may hear that birth centers are a cross between home and hospital, therefore somehow safer than home. The truth is, there is no difference in the skill level of freestanding birth center midwives or emergency equipment available, than would be available at home.
It is always recommended to interview out of hospital midwives thoroughly. Through the list of interview questions below, you will be able to see the benefits of the Midwifery Model of Care and determine if it is right for you.

SOME QUESTIONS TO ASK

- What are your credentials?

- How long have you been practicing?

- Do you work with a partner and do you have adequate backup?

- Who else will be there to assist you at my birth?

- Will you be away any time during my 37-42 week window? (I actually would include your first week of postpartum as well making it a *37-43 week window!*) You want the midwife or midwifery team that you hired to attend your birth.

- What are your statistics for transferring to the hospital? (this should be around 10-15%)

- What is your cesarean rate? (it should be around 5%)

- Can I have references to previous clients?

- What is your license #? (you can research the number to see if there are any issues)

- What is your postpartum care schedule? (the typical schedule is: a visit on day 1, 3, 5 or 6, 1-2 visits in week 2, a 3 or 4 week visit, and a final 6 week visit.)

- If I have postpartum issues, will you come more often? (the answer should be, "Yes, either myself or my assistant will come as often as needed.")

HOSPITAL BIRTH CENTER

The hospital birth center used to be called the labor and delivery unit. Many hospitals changed the name sometime in the 1980's to appeal to patients that desired a more natural birth environment and experience as the out of hospital birth movement was growing rapidly.
Hospitals always use the medical model of care and practice risk management, even when midwives are providing the care. In the US, your hospital birth may be attended by either a CNM, an obstetrician, or a family practice MD. Nurse midwives are only allowed to attend the low risk births. If you become high risk during the labor and birth process, your care will be taken over by the attending OB. *Not all hospitals have midwives on staff.* If you are curious about having a midwife attend your hospital birth, inquire with your care team.

THINGS TO CONSIDER WHEN CHOOSING YOUR HOSPITAL

- Is it a teaching hospital? Teaching hospitals can be good if you have a high-risk pregnancy and need the latest medical technology. If you give birth in a teaching hospital, you will be seen by resident medical students who are overseen by the attending obstetrician and all final decisions are made after the student gets permission to move forward from the attending OB. One important thing to know about teaching hospitals is that you will have more bodies in the room observing your birth, which you may or may not be comfortable with. You may be faced with being evaluated by the student, followed by the attending OB, which means that there may be more face to face time with providers, which can interrupt your labor flow. If this does not sound appealing to you, consider asking for limited student contact in your birth plan.

- Are there midwives on staff? If so how many, and what shifts are covered by them? Some hospitals have midwives, but they only are on day shifts, or limited times throughout the week.

- Is the hospital considered a Mother Friendly Hospital or a Baby Friendly Hospital? If not, what do they offer similarly?

Check out the mother and baby friendly hospital Initiatives here:
https://www.babyfriendlyusa.org/
http://www.motherfriendly.org/

HIRING AN OBSTETRICIAN OR CERTIFIED NURSE MIDWIFE

IF YOUR PROVIDER OF CHOICE IS IN PRIVATE PRACTICE, QUESTIONS TO ASK

- Will you be away any time during my 37-42 week window? (or 37-43 week window)

- If so, who is your backup provider?

- Does your backup provider have the same practice style and philosophies as you?

- Will I get to meet the backup provider at some point during my pregnancy?

IF YOUR PROVIDER IS IN GROUP PRACTICE, QUESTIONS TO ASK

- What percentage of your clients' births do you attend?

- Can we meet the other practice partners that could possibly be at our birth at some point in our pregnancy?

- Do the others in your practice have the same style and philosophies?

THE FARM

Expecting families travel from all over the world to experience birth at The Farm in Tennessee. The Farm, an out of hospital birth location was established in 1970 and has become an institution for natural birth for low risk families. Their statistics are stellar with less than 2% Cesarean rate. The Farm has been a refuge for birthing people who have been denied the type of births they desire, such as: breech, twins and VBAC. The Farm midwives have a process for selecting good candidates for births with their midwives based on health status, emotional well being, will, and determination.

More info: http://thefarmmidwives.org/

NOTES:

MAJOR PLAYERS IN THE HORMONAL COCKTAIL OF LABOR AND BIRTH

PROGESTERONE

- Maintains pregnancy

- Reduces pregnant person's immunologic response to the fetus

- Causes nausea in pregnancy

- Released by placenta in pregnancy

- Relaxes smooth muscle, preventing uterine contractions during pregnancy

- Decreases gastrointestinal movement to aide in higher absorption of nutrients in pregnancy

OXYTOCIN

- Facilitates uterine contractions

- Aides in bonding and attachment

- Creates an altered state of consciousness

- Aides in milk letdown reflex during breastfeeding

- Relaxation helps release oxytocin

- Epinephrine and stress slow down oxytocin release

- Quiet, privacy, and darkness aide in altered state of consciousness, bonding, and oxytocin release in labor and birth

- Adequate oxytocin release reduces postpartum bleeding after birth by contracting the uterus

- Pitocin is synthetic oxytocin

ENDORPHIN

- Nature's morphine

- Pain relief

- Relaxation

- Aides in altered state of consciousness in labor

- Aides in bonding and dependence between birthing person and baby post birth

EPINEPHRINE

- Stress hormone in flight or fight response

- Can slow down or stop labor

- At the end of first stage labor a large release of epinephrine aides in energizing for the pushing phase and wakes laboring person and baby up for the bonding period immediately post birth

NOTES:

USING THE SENSE OF TOUCH IN LABOR

Touch is one of the most potent tools that we can use to alleviate the intense sensations of labor and birth. Touch works on a very deep level to relax, comfort, and communicate love and safety. There are many different ways to touch a person in labor.

EFFLEURAGE: Light, circular touch on the body. You can lightly rub any part of a laboring person's body to help calm them. Most people who enjoy effleurage in labor will appreciate it applied to the back, legs, and belly.

FIRM, STEADY PRESSURE: Touch in labor works with the nervous system to help block pain messages. Because of this, it is important to maintain the touch that you are using throughout contractions. For partners, if you are wondering if the pressure that you are using is pleasurable, simply ask for feedback in between contractions using simple yes or no questions. For those who are in labor, communicate your touch receptivity through non-verbal or verbal communication.

MASSAGE: During labor, a nice neck or head massage can help put her/him/them into a deep relaxing state and promote the release of endorphin and oxytocin.

HOLDING HANDS AND/OR FEET: Sometimes effleurage, firm pressure, and massage are just too stimulating to the laboring person. She/he/they will need to focus so intensely on their work that your touch can be a distraction. If this is the case, simply hold their hands or feet. This can also alleviate pain and promote relaxation.

GATE CONTROL THEORY

There are "gates" in the nervous system that can be open or closed to pain signals. There is strong evidence that shows when a person is being touched, those "gates" close to pain signals, actually preventing them from reaching the brain. Other things that can help alleviate pain by closing the "gates" to pain signals are:

- Touch

- Vocalization

- Submersion in water

- Positive thoughts and affirmations

When working with a doula or extra labor support, they can provide massage while the partner stays close and emotionally supports you through your contractions.

SACRAL COUNTERPRESSURE

As the baby moves down, the joints in your pelvis will begin to stretch and the pelvic bones will start to open. This usually causes discomfort in the lower back and in your joints around the sacrum. Your labor support team can help greatly reduce discomfort in this area by applying counterpressure to the sacral area.

You may find yourself needing this type of touch later in your active phase of labor, once the baby is engaged, but it can feel good anytime.

The sacrum is easy to find. Just place your hand in the middle of the lower back and you are on the sacrum. You can actually feel the hard shelf of bone when you push down. You can try either putting firm, steady pressure on this area during contractions, or rubbing up and down with either light or firm pressure during contractions. She/he/they will let you know what pressure feels best.

It also feels very good to have firm, steady pressure on either side of the sacrum during contractions, as pictured here. Lean down with your body's weight instead of using your arm muscles while giving this pressure and remember not to stop until the contraction is over unless she/he/they ask you to.

Sometimes she/he/they will want more pressure than you can give with your hands. Try using fists or elbows if this is the case. The knee press is also helpful in relieving lower back pressure. Simply press directly toward the back of the chair on the bottom of your partner's knee caps.

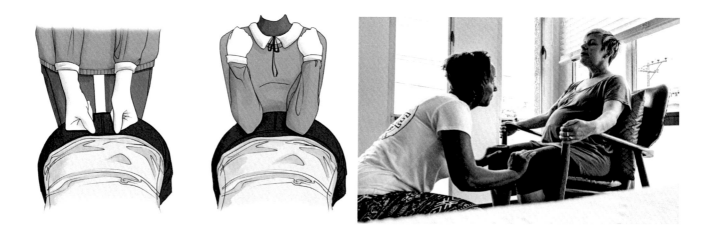

When labor is so intense that counterpressure and massage is not wanted, hold hands or feet. This is incredibly grounding and helps relieve pain by closing the gates.

TOUCH RELAXATION

"The Messenger of Allah (peace be upon him) once asked me to massage his waist. When I began massaging the back, accidentally my fingers touched the Seal of Prophethood." (Shamail Muhammadiyah)

"I did not see anyone who more resembled the Messenger of Allah, may Allah bless him and grant him peace, in manner of speaking than Fatima. When she came to him, he stood up for her, made her welcome, kissed her and had her sit in his place. When the Prophet came to her, she stood up for him, took his hand, made him welcome, kissed him, and made him sit in her place. She came to him during his final illness and he greeted her and kissed her." (Al-Adab Al-Mufrad)

The Messenger of Allah (peace be upon him) said: "No two Muslims meet each other and shake hands, except that Allah forgives them before they part." (Jami` at-Tirmidhi)

This relaxation exercise is designed to be practiced with your partner, doula, or a loved one: anyone that you trust who will be an active participant at your birth. The benefits of practicing this relaxation together (we suggest a minimum of once a week):

Touch is bonding. Get your oxytocin and feel good love hormones flowing. Oxytocin is released when we are with people who we love and that care for us in a loving way. Oxytocin is released with loving touch. The baby also reaps benefits whenever his/her birthing parent gets a burst of oxytocin; this oxytocin 'bath' sends a message to the baby that life is safe, and feels good!

With practice, your partner will be more confident in these techniques, so practice them often. The more confident he/she/they are, the more solidly supported you feel and the easier it is to let yourself go deeper into labor's altered state of consciousness. In this space, you can find your focus and rhythm knowing that your labor support is focused on you, your work, and relaxation. Furthermore, when your partner/s and helper/s feel confident in these techniques, they can feel the joy of the birth process, rather than fear and doubt in themselves.

Throughout this course we will be teaching you a variety of touch, pressure, and massage techniques. Labor is a fluid and continually changing process and you will not know what it is that feels relieving or good in labor until you are experiencing it. Your touch preferences can change as quickly as your labor in flow and intensity, so having as many tools ready in your "toolbox" as possible puts you at a great advantage in preparation for your birth experience. Before beginning this practice, make sure your partner is wearing comfortable clothes and has at least 15-20 minutes to focus on this exercise without feeling rushed or needed elsewhere.

If you like, find some music that is relaxing for the both of you. Alternatively you can do this practice without background sounds. Other options are Quran recitation (preferably what you may like to use during labor, you will find the slower recitations to be most relaxing), Tibetan bowls, classical music like mozart, or sounds of the ocean, rain forest, or rain.

When you are through with this relaxation practice, take time to discuss what you liked and what you did not like; which areas that you would have liked your partner to focus on longer and areas that you don't like to be touched. Be sure to also show your partner how you would like him/her/them to adjust so that their touch works best for you.

Get absolutely comfortable in either a sitting or lying position, being supported completely by pillows. Turn off the ringer on your phone and make sure that you are not hungry, thirsty, or needing to use the restroom so that you can be free to fall into a deep relaxing state with no interruptions. It is good to be in a state of wudu. Put on the music if you like, making sure it isn't too loud. As you relax, the music will appear louder, so it's best to start at a lower volume so that it remains relaxing throughout the exercise.

Partners, be aware that this will be a meditative exercise for you as well. Get comfortable and remember to stay present.
Sit in a comfortable position and do the 3 breaths together. This will bring you into your body and prepare you to be present and relaxed.

The Practice:

Bismillah.
Take a moment to center your heart on Allah*. Take deep diaphragmatic (belly) breaths, expanding the centering feelings that you have in your heart with every breath. Breathe in through your nose, feeling your belly rise. Breathe out slowly, emptying all of the air in your lungs by pulling your bellybutton toward your spine. The speed of your breathing is slow, relaxed, natural and comfortable. With each breath out, release tension in your body, surrender, and sink deeper into the pillows or where you lie.

- Take a deep breath in, breathe out and release your head, neck, shoulders, arms, and hands.

- Take a deep breath in, breathe out and release your chest, mid back, torso and belly.

- Take a deep breath in, breathe out and release your legs, hips, ankles and feet.

Take a moment to notice how your body feels. There will be parts that are more relaxed and free of tension than others. Don't try to change anything right now; just notice any discomfort, tight muscles, aches, and pains.

Partners: start with the head, working your way slowly down the body, ending at the feet. Hold a relaxing pressure to each part of her/his/their body with intention and love. Breathe slow diaphragmatic breaths, in for 4 out for 4 and feel the response in your partner's body with each hand/pressure placement. You will use your intuition to guide you in how long to stay with each part of the body and this will be a very good practice for intuitive touch during labor and birth.

Pregnant partners, it is your job to breathe into the areas you are being touched: in for 4 and out for 4 with every placement of your partner's hands. Bring breath in, and release tension with the out breath. Partners end this practice holding the feet with firm, steady pressure until you both feel complete.

THE CORNERSTONE METHOD OF CHILDBIRTH EDUCATION

ENGAGE. INFORM. EMPOWER.

CLASS FIVE

SENSE: SOUND

Today we will be discussing fears and common misconceptions. One of the most useful practices in pregnancy to prepare for a joyful birth is fear release and trust in your body, your baby, and the birth process. The sound sense is all about the messages that you allow in during your pregnancy. Messages, words, thoughts, and stories are very potent and can cause stress or happiness; let the positive in and leave the negative at the door. **Pregnancy is a time of great emotional and psychosomatic vulnerability. It is imperative to surround yourself with positive books, stories, messages, affirmations, community and family members, and care providers.** Take time to research statements that scare you or just don't seem to make sense. Find a trusted and evidence-based source to turn to with questions while staying as far away from fear-based sources as possible.

COMMON MYTHS AND MISCONCEPTIONS:

CHILDBEARING HIPS

How curvy or not curvy, "big boned" or "small boned" a woman or pregnant person appears to be has absolutely no indication to the size and capacity of her/his/their pelvis. The baby travels through the pelvic brim, mid-pelvis, and outlet, which cannot be seen from the outside of the body. The pelvic bones, which make some women more curvy than others, are on the outside of the pelvis and have no correlation to the inner size or capacity of the pelvis.

"YOUR BABY IS TOO BIG FOR YOUR PELVIS."

No one can tell if your baby is too large for your pelvis. Period. This only happens in a very, very rare condition called CPD. Even very large babies make their way through the pelvis because the baby's head has 5 movable plates which can mold and overlap to reduce it's diameter, and the pelvis Pelvis has 4 joints, they are: pubis, (2) sacroiliac, and tail bone. All of which have softened in preparation to expand, shift, and open during labor and birth. . Even if women in your family have had cesareans for CPD (Cephalopelvic Disproportion), there is a good chance you can birth your baby just fine. Find a birth team that believes in you and your pelvis and consider using the Optimal Fetal Positioning techniques that you have learned in this course. The most common reason for babies getting 'stuck' is a malpositioned head, which makes for a larger diameter trying to come through the pelvic bones. These babies most often get un-stuck and are born vaginally with patience, lots of movement, and the support of your birth team behind you.

MY MOTHER, SISTER, OR GRANDMOTHER HAD FAST LABORS, SO MY LABOR WILL ALSO BE FAST.

Sorry to burst that bubble, but your grandmother, mother, and even sister have lived and birthed under different circumstances than you. They lived in a different era, ate different foods, and had different care providers. If this is your first baby, plan on your labor being 24-36 hours. If it is shorter, great! If it is an average labor, you'll be well prepared to get through it.

YOUR PARTNER IS THE ONLY LABOR SUPPORT YOU NEED.

Your partner needs help supporting you, and will need their own support throughout this time. This is also your partner's baby and the birth will be paramount for both of you. While being in the very emotional experience of becoming a parent, partners are expected to hold you up, press on your back, cuddle, monitor the temperature in the room while you are hot, then cold, then hot again, make sure you are eating, drinking, peeing, and comfortable. They are also timing contractions, fielding phone calls from the family, and wondering when it will be time to go to your birthplace or call the midwife. Being the number one support person is exhausting. Furthermore, it is impossible to fully relax and enjoy being in the experience of the birth of their baby when your partner is making sure that everything is taken care of. Taking on this role when running on 24-36 hours with no sleep, or more is not sustainable.
Hiring a doula or having a trusted friend who is familiar with birth and can help without disrupting or bringing their own agenda into the birth room changes this whole picture.
Your support person knows a lot about labor and birth. They are well rested and can be used as a pillar of strength, an information bank, physical and emotional support, and an advocate. With an extra support person in the room, your partner is also supported, and can eat, stay hydrated, get little breaks, and focus on supporting you and baby with love, snuggles, and calm energy. You want your partner to be taken care of so that they are fully present for you and baby, and you are both left with a lifelong memory that this was the best day, or 3, of your lives.

BEING 35 OR OLDER AUTOMATICALLY PUTS ME INTO A HIGH RISK CATEGORY.

Nope. You are not high risk unless you have a serious illness or health condition.

THE CORD AROUND BABY'S NECK IS AN EMERGENCY.

We have an innate panic reaction to hearing about cords wrapped around baby's neck. The truth is that 60% of all babies are born with cords around their necks, bodies, legs, feet, under their arms, and around their bodies. Cords can get wrapped around baby's body parts, sometimes even two or three times. During the birth process, baby is getting oxygen straight through the cord into their bloodstream and they won't use their lungs until their body is born and they take their first breath. Fun fact: the vessels in the umbilical cord have a protective jelly like substance surrounding and cushioning them so that the cord can get wrapped around baby, or even have a knot and still carry out their oxygen carrying functions. In a normal birth, the cord will not strangle the baby from simply being wrapped around its neck. Yes, cord accidents can happen, but they are rare because there are protective mechanisms in place.

FEAR BASED SOURCES INCLUDE

- "A Baby Story" TV series

- Any other reality TV show about birth

- Books that are long lists of what you should not do or cannot do

- Anyone who tries to tell you a scary or negative story about birth

We recommend all of the <u>Sears and Sears</u> books for use as your reference library.

Let's explore some of the common statements you may read or hear from well-meaning friends, coworkers, family or community members, and/or your care provider(s).

Write down any fears that you have about the pregnancy, birth, or postpartum here:

Partner, write down any of your fears about pregnancy, birth, or postpartum here:

LABOR POSITIONS:

The most important thing to remember about labor positions is to listen to your body and your baby. Not everyone needs direction to find the "right" position. Staying relaxed as possible is the key. When you feel an urge to move, move. Try slow dancing, rocking, sitting on a birth ball, or being on your hands and knees. When lying on your side, remember to use pillows between your knees to support your back and make room for the baby to move down.

All positions should facilitate relaxation during and in between contractions. The more relaxed you are in between contractions, the more energy will be conserved for the duration of labor and birth. Partners, follow the laboring person's lead and support them with pillows, connection, and touch. Dozing in between contractions may happen, and this is a great bonus. There is no need to wake up if you find yourself falling asleep intermittently.

Hands and knees position offers a great opportunity to receive counterpressure and lower back massage during and in between contractions. Always make sure to stay as relaxed as possible, and try not to hold yourself up with your wrists. Leaning over a chair, bed, or ball is a great way to be relaxed in this position.

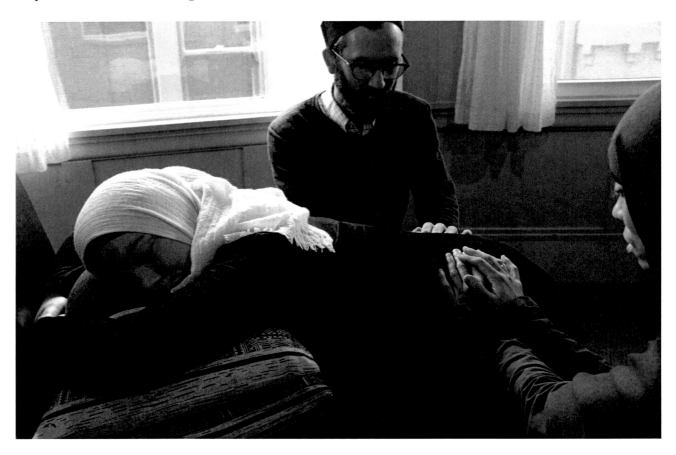

If you find that squatting is difficult on your own, your partner or doula can help you get into a good squat position with what we call "the supported squat".

GETTING INTO A SUPPORTED SQUAT

- Partner sits in a chair without arms with their seat at the edge of the chair

- Laboring person squats down with their back to partner

- Partner supports the laboring person's body with their legs

- Laboring person relaxes into the position, being fully supported

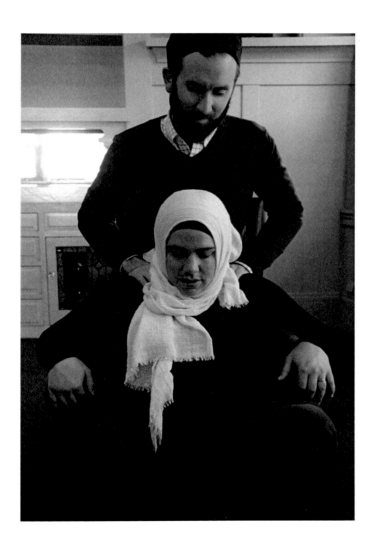

Straddling your partner is another variation of the supported squat. Your partner can help open your pelvis by letting your bottom sag between their legs.

You can also get the same benefit from sitting on the toilet. The toilet puts you in a perfect squat position and you are already accustomed to letting your pelvic floor go here. Straddling the toilet also gives your support team easy access to your lower back for counterpressure and massage.

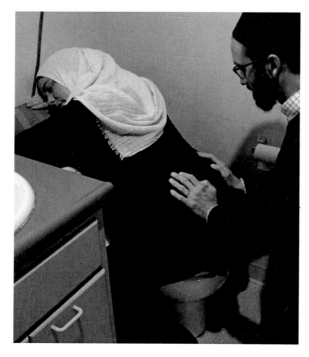

If you have access to a yoga chair, you can use it to support your body in a squat position.

The birth ball can be used for being in a relaxed hands and knees position, as well as leaning, sitting and rocking, and countless other positions. Your course leader will discuss these positions in class.

The peanut ball is an excellent tool to help make room for baby and is shown to speed labors. It is also a great way to open the hips when laboring with an epidural.

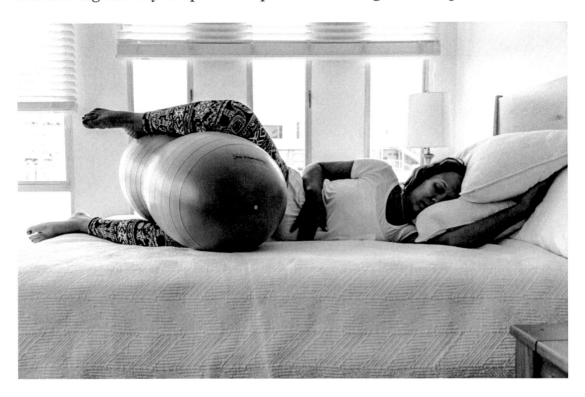

NOTES:

HOMEWORK FOR NEXT WEEK
RESEARCH PROJECT AND PRESENTATION

Next week's class is all about interventions and procedures. Your trainer will assign one of these topics for you to research, and you will be giving a presentation on this topic to the class.

YOUR ASSIGNED PROCEDURE OR INTERVENTION:

INFORMATION TO GATHER AND PRESENT

- Indications (why would it be proposed or performed?)

- Description of the procedure

- Benefits of the intervention

- Risks of the intervention

- Alternatives to the intervention

- Prevalence rates of this particular intervention at the location that you have chosen to deliver

GUIDELINES

Information should be evidence-based and up to date. Please find at least three sources to cite and be prepared to answer questions about your topic. You will be given ten minutes to present. We recommend practicing a couple times during the week. Some people like to bring in slides or handouts. While these are happily accepted, they are not required.

If you have any difficulty with finding information or any questions, please feel free to contact your trainer.

YOUR COURSE LEADER'S CONTACT INFO:

SOUND RELAXATION

> "Allah is the Light of the heavens and the earth. The similitude of His light is as a niche wherein is a lamp. The lamp is in a glass. The glass is of a starlike brilliance. (This lamp is) kindled from a blessed tree, an olive neither eastern nor western, whose oil would almost glow forth (of itself) though no fire touched it. Light upon light, Allah guides unto His light whom He wills. And Allah speaks to mankind in parables, and Allah is knower of all things." (Surah An-Nur (#24), Ayah 35)
>
> The Prophet (peace be upon him) supplicated: "O Allah, place light in my heart, light in my tongue, light in my hearing, light in my eyesight, light on my right hand, light on my left hand, light in front of me, light behind me, light below me, O Allah, give me abundant light." (Sunan Abi Dawud)

This relaxation exercise will combine relaxing sounds with a guided visualization. We recommend the sounds you choose to be calming and without distracting words so that it doesn't take your focus from your visualization. Through practice, your brain and heart will automatically start filling you with light and relaxation when you hear these sounds. The more you practice this script, the more automatic relaxation will come to you when you put it into practice. This is a simple concept that is used in many meditation practices around the world.

Get absolutely comfortable in either a sitting or lying position, being supported completely by pillows. Turn off the ringer on your phone and make sure that you are not hungry, thirsty, or needing to use the restroom so that you can be free to fall into a deep relaxing state with no interruptions. It is good to be in a state of wudu.

Have a partner or friend read this script to you. As they read, have them pause for one minute in between each statement. When the reader gets to the end of the script, they can quietly sneak out and leave you to continue your relaxation until you are ready to come out of it. If you would prefer to do this practice on your own, simply record yourself reading this script and play it back once you are nice and comfortable.

After a couple of practices, it will be easy to pull this visualization scene up in your mind without any help inshaAllah (God willing). This is precisely why we recommend you practice relaxation and visualization often in preparation for childbirth, so that your body can find a place of deep relaxation without any effort while you do the work of bringing your baby into this world.

The Practice:

Bismillah.
Take a moment to center your heart on Allah*. Take deep diaphragmatic (belly) breaths, expanding the centering feelings that you have in your heart with every breath. Breathe in through your nose, feeling your belly rise. Breathe out slowly, emptying all of the air in your lungs by pulling your bellybutton toward your spine. The speed of your breathing is slow, relaxed, natural and comfortable. With each breath out, release tension in your body, surrender, and sink deeper into the pillows or where you lie.

- Take a deep breath in, breathe out and release your head, neck, shoulders, arms, and hands.

- Take a deep breath in, breathe out and release your chest, mid back, torso and belly.

- Take a deep breath in, breathe out and release your legs, hips, ankles and feet.

Imagine you are in a room. This room is the embodiment of comfort and safety. The room has the perfect temperature and lighting, and your favorite relaxing music is playing. You are so comfortable and relaxed right where you are. Picture your perfect comfy bed, chair, hammock, etc. that you are in.

The room is all yours, and no one is allowed to knock or come in until you want company, so know that you will not be interrupted. This is your time.

Imagine a brilliant, white light*** in front of your chest. Picture this light as a warm beam, coming on to your chest and entering your heart. As you breathe, envision that light slowly filling your body, starting with your lungs, and slowly filling your belly, head and limbs. The brilliant, warm, white light travels down your body, filling every single cell as it moves. Each breath brings more light into your body radiating out from your illuminated heart. This light is life affirming and calming, filling you with a sense of wellbeing and safety. All is well and as it should be. Each breath you take brings oxygen filled with this calming, loving light to you and your baby.

Imagine the light traveling down your arms to your fingertips. It fills your head. See your uterus and baby filling up with this light and you both feel nothing but calm, relaxation, and love. The light now fills your lower body and legs.

Light continues to fill your body, ankles, feet and toes.

The light now fills your whole body, your whole being. It overflows and travels out the bottom of your feet and the top of your head. It flows out the sides of your body and your hands. It expands to surround your whole body, enclosing you and the baby in its purity, love, and protection. You are completely relaxed and feel trust, love, and safety.

Keep breathing and hold the image of this light for as long as is needed. When you are complete, you can slowly come out of your relaxation, feeling energized and peaceful.

Footnotes:

***Alternate visualizations to that of light: energy, positivity, trust, the warmth of mercy or compassion, the experience of the manifestation of His names...

THE CORNERSTONE METHOD OF CHILDBIRTH EDUCATION

ENGAGE. INFORM. EMPOWER.

CLASS SIX

SENSE: VOICE

YOUR VOICE is essential in your pregnancy, labor, birth, postpartum, and beyond. Voice your needs to your partner, family, community members, and care providers. Now is the time to practice advocating for yourself and your baby, as this is something you will be doing for the rest of your lives together. Every day parents need to advocate, make tough decisions, and communicate with their families, communities, and children. The time to start is now.

SOME QUESTIONS TO EXPLORE:

Answers may be different for you both. Let this be a practice in opening lines of communication together and gaining a stronger understanding of each other's needs and wishes.

- What do you want for your birth?

- What is the most important factor in your birth experience?

- What do you need from each other?

- How can you and your partner or community members show up for each other in building and supporting this new family?

B.R.A.I.N.

A COMMON SENSE APPROACH TO DECISION MAKING

B: BENEFITS   What are the benefits of this proposed intervention or procedure?

R: RISKS   What are the risks of this proposed intervention or procedure?

A: ALTERNATIVES   Are there any possible alternatives to this proposed intervention or procedure?

I: INTUITION   What does your gut tell you?

N: NEED TIME   If it isn't an emergency, take some time to discuss the proposed intervention or procedure and make a decision.

QUESTIONS TO ASK

- Is this an emergency?

- Please explain all the risks, benefits, and alternatives available.

- What if we don't? What if we wait?

- We need some time alone to discuss this.

A NEW PARADIGM IN SURGICAL BIRTH

- Family Centered Cesarean Project

- The Gentle Cesarean

- The Natural Cesarean Technique

This new surgical birth movement has been created to help the birthing person and baby through a cesarean section in a gentler, more natural way. Some hospitals are open to exploring these proposed methods including: slow delivery, lowering of the curtain for delivery, delayed cord clamping, skin-to-skin contact and nursing in the operating room. Employing these measures can greatly improve the birthing person's experience of their birth and enhance bonding with baby, including higher rates of breastfeeding success and less postpartum depression.

The process of slow delivery, which mimics the vaginal squeeze, can greatly reduce the need for baby to need suctioning and resuscitation immediately post birth, which in turn reduces length of separation of parents and baby.
Consumers can help this movement become a permanent and widely accessible option by discussing this with and requesting it of their care providers.

Please use the links below to learn more about this style of cesarean section:
http://thedoulaguide.blogspot.com/2012/12/the-natural-cesarean_9.html

NOTES:

EXPECTATION, OUTCOME, AND COMMUNITY

It is absolutely reasonable to expect a healthy pregnancy and birth. It is equally reasonable to expect that your classmates will have the same experience, and in most cases you will all have healthy outcomes.

The Cornerstone Method childbirth education classes are more than just childbirth preparation for the immediate family. We intend to foster and expand community through these courses. You will be getting to know your classmates' hopes, dreams, and fears about becoming parents. You will also be sharing deep feelings and experiencing joyous, bonding moments together. After everyone has had their babies, you will all get together for a reunion to support one another, share a meal, and your birth experiences. Because these classes help create special bonds between and within groups of participants, you and your classmates may go on to have weekly, monthly, or even yearly get-togethers; this is your new community.

When in community, we are healthier as individuals and as a society in body, mind, and spirit, and this is why Cornerstone helps foster this community dynamic. Sometimes in life there are bumps in the road and unexpected bad outcomes, and this also happens in birth. When there is an unexpected outcome with one of our students or your classmates, Cornerstone does what we can to support you and them. There can be unwanted cesareans, long hospital stays, unexpected intervention, and in rare events, loss.

It is a well-known fact that when someone experiences the loss of a baby, they can be shut out and isolated from the support of their community.

WHAT TYPICALLY HAPPENS

1. They feel so heartbroken that it is impossible to reach out.

2. The people in their community that have children feel guilty about being in a happy and blissful stage of their lives and that it just wouldn't be right to reach out, as their happy situation would "just make the family feel worse."

3. Friends feel like it's best to leave care and support to the immediate family and professionals and will wait to be contacted by the family for support, giving everyone the space that they think is needed.

4. We as a culture don't know how to support, or what we have to offer when there is a loss of a baby. We may feel that we are not equipped and fear that we may make a mistake, so we stay away.

Your Cornerstone course leader will contact you and ask that you be a part of an effort to help if there is a loss among your peers. This will most likely be in the form of sending flowers, a signed card, and organizing a meal train. Depending on your relationship to the family, you may take on a more active support role. When someone experiences a loss, we do not wait for them to ask for help. Most often they are unable to even think of what is needed, or they do not have the wherewithal to reach out and ask. Food is the best way to send love and help nourish the family in body, mind, and spirit.

The Sunnah of the Prophet Muhammad (peace be upon him) encourages this beautiful custom: "When the news of the death of Ja'far came, the Prophet said: 'Prepare some food for the family of Ja'far, for indeed something has happened to them that will keep them busy.'" (Jami` at-Tirmidhi)

This is a wonderful blog post with resources, as well as a podcast interview with Amy Wright Glenn: birth doula, hospital chaplain, founder of The Institute for the Study of Birth, Breath, and Death, and the creator of Holding Space for Pregnancy Loss trainings. http://www.birthful.com/podcaststillbirth/

The podcast covers topics such as:

- Why we should be talking more about this

- When birth and death collide

- How to best help moms/birthing people – the presence of listening

- The importance of a "teach me" perspective instead of a "fix it" perspective

- Ways to honor the baby and acknowledge the loss

NOTES:

NOTES FROM TODAY'S PRESENTATIONS:

VOCALIZATION SKILLS PRACTICE EXERCISE

Hold an uncomfortable yoga position (Thai goddess or squat) for the duration of a short contraction (one minute). Start with holding this minute long pose **without using any relaxation techniques** and simply note your physical and emotional responses. Try holding this pose a second time with your eyes closed and focus on relaxing key tension points (eyes, forehead, jaw, shoulders, belly). When you begin to feel uncomfortable, start to make **deep, low, om sounds.** Practice your deep breathing while vocalizing. Try holding one last pose and vocalize through the **entire minute**, making **even louder, deeper om sounds.** Note the differences in your experience with each practice. Record these observations and discuss.

FIRST POSE PHYSICAL AND EMOTIONAL RESPONSES

SECOND POSE PHYSICAL AND EMOTIONAL RESPONSES

THIRD POSE PHYSICAL AND EMOTIONAL RESPONSES

VOICE RELAXATION

"Allah has revealed the most beautiful message, a Book consistent in its verses yet repeating its teachings in different ways. Those who fear their Lord are filled with awe when they hear it, their skins and their hearts become soft to the remembrance of Allah." (Surah Az-Zumar Ayah 23)

"The first of what the Messenger of Allah (peace be upon him) initiated with of Prophethood, when Allah wanted to honor him and grant His mercy upon His creatures, was that he would not see anything (in a dream) except that it would occur like the break of dawn. So he continued upon that for as long as Allah willed for him to continue, and seclusion was made beloved to him, such that there was not anything more beloved to him than being alone." (Jami` at-Tirmidhi)

Our breath is one of the most effective relaxation tools that we possess. All relaxation and meditation techniques have breath in common. Breathing is automatic; we go through the day without thinking about it. We do however, from time to time feel stressed, and in this state tend to take shallower shorter breaths, not fully exhaling. Most of us have a built-in response to these moments that makes us take deep breaths to calm ourselves in stressful situations. Our bodies know that it is difficult to be stressed or panicked when we are taking deep, slow breaths, filling our lungs with oxygen, and slowly releasing until our lungs are completely empty.

Deep breathing:

- Calms the nervous system

- Releases good feeling neuro-chemicals in the brain

- Relaxes the muscles

- Lowers blood pressure

- Activates our parasympathetic nervous system, or "rest and digest" (benefits our digestive system)

Before Starting:

Get absolutely comfortable in either a sitting or lying position, being supported completely by pillows. Turn off the ringer on your phone and make sure that you are not hungry, thirsty, or needing to use the restroom so that you can be free to fall into a deep relaxing state with no interruptions. It is good to be in a state of wudu.

Have a partner or friend read this script to you. As they read, have them pause for one minute in between each statement. When the reader gets to the end of the script, they can quietly sneak out and leave you to continue your relaxation until you are ready to come out of it. If you would prefer to do this practice on your own, simply record yourself reading the script and play it back once you are nice and comfortable.

The Practice:

Bismillah.
Take a moment to center your heart on Allah*. Take deep diaphragmatic (belly) breaths, expanding the centering feelings that you have in your heart with every breath. Breathe in through your nose, feeling your belly rise. Breathe out slowly, emptying all of the air in your lungs by pulling your bellybutton toward your spine. The speed of your breathing is slow, relaxed, natural and comfortable. With each breath out, release tension in your body, surrender, and sink deeper into the pillows or where you lie.

- Take a deep breath in, breathe out and release your head, neck, shoulders, arms, and hands.

- Take a deep breath in, breathe out and release your chest, mid back, torso and belly.

- Take a deep breath in, breathe out and release your legs, hips, ankles and feet.

Now that you are relaxed and your nervous system begun to calm itself, bring your awareness to your breathing. Is it shallow, fast, slow, or deep? Do a quick scan of your body, noticing any areas that are tense or sore. How does your stomach feel? Are you stressed about anything from the day?

Now take a controlled, full breath in through your nose until your lungs are completely full of air. Breathe from the diaphragm. You will feel your belly rise. Notice how refreshing it is to get a full deep breath in. Exhale through your mouth slowly, until your lungs have completely emptied.

Repeat: Inhale in through your nose slowly, relaxing the diaphragm to make room for your lungs to expand and fill with oxygen. Again: Exhale through your mouth slowly, until your lungs have completely emptied.

Let your body decide when to take the next deep diaphragmatic breath and when to exhale.

Keep breathing in, and out slowly and completely. While you are breathing, do another complete body scan, from head to toe. Are the tense areas softening? Focus on releasing any tension you find with your exhalation.

Scan Your Body:

- The top of your head

- Forehead

- Jaw

- Neck

- Shoulders

- Chest

- Arms and hands

- Torso

- Belly

- Back

- Low back

- Hips & buttocks

- Thighs

- Knees

- Calves

- Ankles

- Feet & toes

Now feel how your body and mind have responded to relaxation. Stay in this deep, restful, calm, and oxygenated state as long as feels comfortable.

Note: Use this breathing technique any time, anywhere. Try practicing taking these breaths a couple times once per hour throughout the day to make sure that you are as relaxed as possible.

THE CORNERSTONE METHOD OF CHILDBIRTH EDUCATION

ENGAGE. INFORM. EMPOWER.

CLASS SEVEN

SENSE: SIGHT

SET YOUR SIGHT ON YOUR MOST DESIRED BIRTH EXPERIENCE AND MAP YOUR WAY TO ITS DESTINATION.

BIRTH PLAN WRITING WORKSHOP

EFFECTIVE BIRTH PLAN GUIDELINES

- One page in length

- No absolutes. Your birth plan should convey flexibility. These are preferences, not demands.

- Try using bullet points and use **bold** typeface for the most important points.

- Write the plan in easy to understand terms, that are in chronological order: labor, birth, postpartum.

- Avoid implications of unethical behavior. Ex: "I would like to avoid an unnecessary cesarean section."

- List those who you plan to have attend the birth: family members, friends, doula, etc.

PERSONAL STATEMENT

Start your birth plan with a short personal statement.   This statement should be no longer than one short paragraph and will start with a short thank you to your providers for the care that you have received thus far. Add three specific things that you have appreciated about your care, then state your intention for your birth in your own words. Ex: unmedicated with doula, medicated, etc.

PERSONAL STATEMENT BRAINSTORM

List three things that you have enjoyed about or during prenatal care:

_____

_____

_____

List your three most important wishes for your birth experience:

_____

_____

_____

PUT THEM TOGETHER INTO A SHORT STATEMENT

Now that your personal statement is written, you can start to list your preferences. It is recommended to preface your preference list with a statement that reads, " All preferences come with the understanding that we want you to do whatever is necessary in the event of an emergency. Thank you for your time and understanding."

PREFERENCE BRAINSTORM

LABOR

We plan to have _____ in attendance. List all family members, friends, doula, etc.

Laboring person's preferred gender pronouns

_____

We are hoping to achieve a(n)_____ birth.

☐ Unmedicated vaginal

☐ Medicated vaginal with the option of analgesics, epidural anesthetic, or nitrous oxide.

☐ Scheduled labor induction

☐ Schedule cesarean delivery

☐ Please provide full informed consent for all proposed procedures and interventions and allow some time alone to discuss options before making our decision.

☐ We would like to have all female care providers when possible.

☐ We would like to have a sign placed on our door saying that men may not enter unless they have permission.

PLEASE LIMIT

☐ Observers: please no residents or students in the birth room

☐ Vaginal exams: as few as possible, and only with consent.

☐ Noise and light

☐ Unnecessary removal of my clothing.

☐ Fetal monitoring: only intermittent unless otherwise indicated and would like the option for mobile telemetry if available.

☐ Offers for medication: we know our options; please do not tempt us by offering.

SECOND STAGE

☐ We would prefer hot compresses, rather than perineal massage.

☐ I would like to push in any position that feels comfortable.

☐ We would like peace and quiet during the pushing phase, please only offer verbal encouragement if I request it.

☐ If I have an epidural, I would like to turn the medication down or off during the pushing phase.

☐ My partner would like the option to help catch the baby

IN THE EVENT OF A SURGICAL BIRTH

☐ Please allow _____ as in-room support during the procedure.

☐ I would like the curtain to be lowered during the delivery.

☐ I would like to have skin-to-skin contact with the baby as soon as possible.

☐ I would like to nurse the baby during the repair phase of surgery.

☐ If baby has to go to the nursery _____ will accompany him/her.

☐ We would like the option of "seeding" the baby after the procedure (GBS -)

☐ Double layer repair

☐ If the baby has been taken to the nursery or any separation has happened, we would like to be reunited as soon as possible. Please delay any routine exams or tests so that we can take advantage of the bonding period.

POSTPARTUM

☐ Please allow time for natural delivery of placenta with no pulling of the cord.

☐ I would prefer to not have a shot of Pitocin after the baby is born unless there is a problem with bleeding.

☐ Please allow for _____ minutes delay before clamping and cutting the cord.

☐ Please limit talking until after the call to prayer (athan) has been performed in the babies ears.

☐ Please do not call out the sex of the baby; we would like to discover this on our own.

☐ Please delay any routine procedures for one and a half hours bonding time.

☐ Please ask for explicit consent before performing any routine procedures on the baby, including bathing.

☐ We will decline Erythromycin ointment.

☐ Please do not bathe the baby.

☐ We would like the baby to stay skin to skin with mother/birthing person during all routine procedures, no separation unless it is an emergency.

☐ We would like to take the placenta home.

☐ I plan to exclusively breastfeed. Please no supplements, formula, or pacifiers.

☐ We do not plan to circumcise.

☐ We plan to delay circumcision until day _____.

NOTES:

GETTING READY FOR THE BIG DAY

FOOD FOR LABOR

When in labor you may only want sweet foods or savory. You won't know which you will favor until you go into labor, so you should have your home well stocked in preparation. If possible, you may also want to have enough to share with your support team (doula, midwives, friends, etc.)

RECOMMENDED FOODS

- Good fats

- Protein

- Bone broth or chicken stock

- Miso soup

- Full fat plain yogurt – you can add a little honey or maple syrup to taste

- Blended coconut milk with dates for sweetness and energy. Bananas or berries are optional for flavor.

- Scrambled eggs

- Toast

- Bananas

- Dates

- Applesauce

- Coconut water

- Water with electrolytes

- Tea

FOODS TO AVOID

- Refined sugar

- Citrus foods and acidic fruits

- Soy protein isolates

- Sugary sports drinks

REMEMBER

In early labor you should be eating throughout, as you will still feel hungry. Once active labor begins, it will be up to your support team to feed you bites of food for energy and sips of fluid for hydration between contractions.

SHOPPING LIST:

PACKING FOR BIRTH

If you are having a homebirth, your midwife will have a list of supplies that you will need to have ready. If you are delivering in the hospital, they will most likely give you a checklist of what to pack. Below are some ideas of things that you will want to have packed and ready to go once you're in your due month:

☐ Change of clothes for you and partner. Choose light, comfortable, easy to put on, easy to nurse in and put the baby skin to skin on your chests in. Make a plan for clothing in the birthing pool, tub, or shower, and for prayer (a rock or dust containing item for performing Tayammum may also come in handy). Remember, all clothing may get soiled or lost, and wearing the clothing they provide in the hospital is optional.

☐ Toiletries: toothbrush and toothpaste, hair ties, chap stick, deodorant, and any other hygiene items that you may need.

☐ Three outfits for baby, including a blanket for when you take baby home

☐ Diapers

☐ Snacks

☐ Phone chargers

☐ Slippers, Non-skid and convenient for wudu

☐ Birth plan (at least 10 copies)

☐ Dua, or Quranic verses to read or display

☐ Birth ball or peanut ball with washable cover

☐ Aromatherapy

☐ Massage apparatus – tennis ball, etc.

☐ Ipod dock or battery operated CD player

☐ Battery operated LED tea lights

☐ Rice sock and cold pack

☐ Any other comfort items

Pack your car for the birth before you go into labor. You'll want two towels, a basin for vomit, and a pillow and blanket. Try getting into different labor positions in the car so that you know where you'll be most comfortable when it's time to go to the hospital. It's a good idea to know which alternate routes are necessary in case you're having to go during rush hour and try a couple "dry runs" at different times of day. Lastly, you'll want to have the car seat in the trunk and know how to attach it properly. The hospital will not allow you to leave with the baby if you don't have a car seat installed.

HOME BIRTH SUPPLY LIST

Your midwife will most likely have a supply list of things for you to gather for the big day. She/he/they may have you order a birth supply kit from a company that is contracted with their practice. These kits are custom-built by your midwife to include supplies that may be needed for the birth. Your midwife will also bring essential medical supplies and equipment to your birth.

AN EXAMPLE OF SUPPLIES FOR HOME BIRTH

FAMILY SUPPLIES TO GATHER

- Towels

- Wash cloths to use for warm compresses

- Old clean sheets for the birth bed

- Flashlight with new batteries

- A small bottle of olive oil

- Garbage bags

- Extra toilet paper

- A medium size plastic or metal mixing bowl known as the "placenta bowl"

- 2-6 quart pan to boil water in

- Extension cord

- Electrolyte mix to add to water or other electrolyte drinks

THE BIRTH SUPPLY KIT
TYPICAL ITEMS

- Underpads (paper/ plastic)

- Sterile gauze

- Sterile gloves

122

- Sterile lubricant packets

- Alcohol Swabs

- Doppler Gel

- Tarp to protect mattress (paper/plastic)

- Herbal Sitz Tea

- Measuring tape (to measure baby)

- Anti Bacterial Wash

- Maternity Pads

- Mesh underwear (to hold maternity pads in place)

- Kneeling Pad

- Foot Printer

- Peri-Bottle

- Cotton infant hats

- "Born at Home" Gift Certificate

SHOPPING LIST:

COMFORT MEASURES TO USE IN LABOR

- Relaxation

- Hypnosis

- Touch

- Massage/counter pressure

- Rebozo

- Postures

- Positions

- Pillows

- Rest

- Movement

- Low lights

- Water – bath and shower

- Music

- Ambiance

- Breathing

- Vocalization

- Birth ball/peanut ball

- Doulas

- Pain medication

List any other comfort measures that you would like to use here:

IDEAS FOR USING A REBOZO

Help support the hands and knees position by pulling upward on the hips.

You can also shimmy the hips back and forth to help relax the lower back and pelvic area.

Pull upward to lengthen the neck and release the muscles in the shoulders:

Water submersion or a shower works wonderfully for relaxation and pain relief. If the tub is big enough, partner can get in and support the laboring person in this relaxing and loving environment. Try lowering the lights and lighting candles or string lights to create a relaxing ambiance. If you're in the hospital, use LED candle lights.

THE LUNGE FOR RELEIVING BACKACHE

If your baby is facing a direction that places extra pressure on your hips or back, try doing lunges during contractions to help the baby make a turn and to relieve the pressure and aches. You can either do these lunges standing or kneeling, depending on your strength and preference.

RELAXATION QUESTIONNAIRE

WHEN I AM STRESSED, I FEEL TENSION IN MY

□ Head

□ Jaw

□ Neck

□ Shoulders

□ Chest

□ Stomach

□ Back

□ Other _____

MY BODY REACTS TO TENSION BY

□ Sweating

□ Heart rate increase

□ Heart pounding or palpitations

□ Difficulty catching my breath

□ Clammy skin

□ Trembling hands or legs

□ "Butterflies" in my stomach

□ Nausea

□ Making a fist

□ Itching/scratching

□ Tapping my feet

□ Biting my nails

☐ Grinding my teeth

☐ Other_____

I can recognize signs of tension in my body by:

I can prevent tension from overwhelming me by:

My partner can help reduce my stress by:

GROUP EXERCISE
THE PILLOW FORTRESS

Break into groups of three: one pregnant person per group and the rest of the team will be support people. Take a stack of pillows and strategically place them everywhere the pregnant person's body will need support. Think of creating a position for her/him/them that helps facilitate maximum relaxation. Your course leader will give you one minute and choose a winning team.

Notes:

HOMEWORK FOR NEXT WEEK'S CLASS

Next week we will be practicing the birth sense joy. There are a few fun exercises that we will be participating in together: including art, dance, and a blessing ceremony. This class will be a potluck, so make sure to let your group and trainer know if you have any dietary restrictions. She/he/they will facilitate the delegation of dishes at the end of your class today.

TO BRING

Bring your dish for the potluck, as well as a bead for each couple in your class. Also, bring a piece of string for the beads that you receive. Your course leader will go over what the bead ceremony and art project entails.

Be prepared to have fun next week!

SIGHT RELAXATION

> Allah's Messenger (peace be upon him) said, "The example of a believer is that of a fresh green plant the leaves of which move in whatever direction the wind forces them to move and when the wind becomes still, it stands straight. Such is the similitude of the believer: He is disturbed by calamities (but is like the fresh plant he regains his normal state soon)..." (Sahih al-Bukhari)

> "And yet others of His signs are the creation of the heavens and the earth, and the difference of your languages and colors; surely there are signs in this for the knowledgeable". (Surah Ar-Rum (#30), Ayah 22)

Today you will explore your relationship with color, by using diaphragmatic breathing and visualization. Every culture has their own relationship to color. Colors are simply waves vibrating at different frequencies. Color has it's own energy. Color has the ability to elicit a range of emotions: calm, excitement, annoyance. It may bring up anger, spark memories, put us in a daydream state, make us hungry, as well as countless other responses.

You may subconsciously or even consciously choose the colors of your wardrobe and what you wear on a daily basis. One day you will want to wear the red shirt. It looks fantastic; it makes you happy. The next day, when you put on the same shirt it just doesn't look or feel right. You choose to put on a different color shirt, and it feels 'right'. You needed vibrancy and energy yesterday, when today you need grounding and confidence.

Breathing in color can have the very same effect as vocalizing and touch. It can activate the gate control response, closing our nervous system's gates to pain messages.

Get absolutely comfortable in either a sitting or lying position, being supported completely by pillows. Turn off the ringer on your phone and make sure that you are not hungry, thirsty, or needing to use the restroom so that you can be free to fall into a deep relaxing state with no interruptions. It is good to be in a state of wudu.

Have a partner or friend read this script to you. As they read, have them pause for a few seconds between each statement. When the reader gets to the end of the script, they can quietly sneak out and leave you to continue your relaxation until you are ready to come out of it. If you would prefer to do this practice on your own, simply record yourself reading the script and play it back once you are nice and comfortable.

The Practice:

Bismillah.
Take a moment to center your heart on Allah*. Take deep diaphragmatic (belly) breaths, expanding the centering feelings that you have in your heart with every breath. Breathe in through your nose, feeling your belly rise. Breathe out slowly, emptying all of the air in your lungs by pulling your bellybutton toward your spine. The speed of your breathing is slow, relaxed, natural and comfortable. With each breath out, release tension in your body, surrender, and sink deeper into the pillows or where you lie.

132

- Take a deep breath in, breathe out and release your head, neck, shoulders, arms, and hands.

- Take a deep breath in, breathe out and release your chest, mid back, torso and belly.

- Take a deep breath in, breathe out and release your legs, hips, ankles and feet.

Choose a color that resonates with you today. Imagine this color as a mist filling the room. This mist comes down into the top of your head as you breathe. See and feel the color filling your body slowly, starting with your head, face, neck and shoulders. The color mist travels down your body, filling up every single cell.

Each breath brings you more color. This color is life affirming and calming. It fills you with a sense of wellbeing and safety. All is well and as it should be. Each breath brings oxygen filled with this color to you and your baby.

Imagine the colored mist traveling down your arms to your fingertips. It is filling your torso.

See your uterus and baby filling up with this color, filling you with calm, trust, and love. The colored mist now fills your lower body and legs. Colored mist continues to fill your body, moving down your ankles, feet, and toes. The colored mist is now filling your whole body, your whole being. It overflows out the bottom of your feet and the top of your head. It flows out the sides of your body and your hands. It expands to surround your whole body; enclosing you and the baby in pure color, love, trust, and protection.

Keep breathing and hold the image of the color for as long as you need. When you are complete, you can slowly come out of your relaxation, feeling energized and peaceful.

THE CORNERSTONE METHOD OF CHILDBIRTH EDUCATION

ENGAGE. INFORM. EMPOWER.

CLASS EIGHT

SENSE: JOY

WHERE AM I THE MOST JOYFUL?

I am with:

I hear:

I see:

I smell:

I feel:

I know:

How can I bring these elements into the birth environment?

AFFIRMATION FLAG ART PROJECT
SOME IDEAS FOR AFFIRMATIONS TO GET THE CREATIVITY FLOWING

PEACE: A POEM BY VIOLETTE GHEMMA MOON RATTLER, AGE 9

Love.
No weapons, no war, just peace
Energy going down you like a waterfall
Sound, magical feeling, we know it all
Let's try to make the world a better place
Love yourself and know that you are loved
That's the secret to peace

BIRTH AFFIRMATIONS AND POSITIVE WORDS

- I am strong

- I can do this

- My body was made to give birth to this baby

- I am supported and loved

- Every contraction brings me closer to the baby

- I am opening

- My cervix blooms open like a rose

- Open

- Love

- Release

- Trust

- Surrender

WHAT TO EXPECT IN THE IMMEDIATE POSTPARTUM

Please make sure to read all of your discharge paperwork carefully, as this information is more about adjustments and not medical information. If you think you are having a medical issue, please contact your provider.

Adjusting to the new family can be very intense and trying. There are ranges of emotions that new parents may go through, and it's important to understand what is in the range of normal.

THE FIRST FEW DAYS

Most people who just gave birth go back and forth from feeling incredibly energized, to feeling like getting hit by a truck. Labor and delivery is hard work and your body needs a lot of rest to heal. When you get those big bursts of energy, try to stay as calm and restful as possible. We recommend staying in or around the bed for at least two weeks post birth and longer if you've had a cesarean section.

For information on Islamic birth traditions and customs please see Appendix A.

THE DAY THREE HORMONE CRASH

The third day postpartum is usually a pretty hard one. Your body is going through an incredible dip in hormones and this is the most intense day. You can expect to feel a range of emotions on the third day including emotional highs and lows, and some possible mild anxiety. This is the day that the milk comes in for a lot of people, as well. Your breasts/chest may be engorged, achy, and full. Stay in the moment and remember that this is very temporary. Your hormones will begin to level out within a day or so and now is the time to relax, breastfeed/chestfeed and bond with your baby. If you have had your placenta processed, this would be a good time to take a capsule to level out those hormones

IDEAS FOR WHAT MAY BE NEEDED

The most difficult task during the immediate postpartum period is cooking and eating. It's a good idea to call on community members, friends, and family to bring over some good food. There are many ways to co-ordinate a "food train". Your doula, or community member can help organize or you can call on a close friend to do so. There are many great online calendars to use. We recommend www.mealtrain.com. You can also have friends and family come over to help, but it's a good idea to let them know in advance what is needed. Baby care comes later. When you are all resting, healing and bonding, friends and family can do some tidying, cooking, errand running or sibling and pet care. Let everyone know what your needs are so that you don't find yourself having to entertain guests. Sleep when the baby sleeps and nurse on demand if you can. If you do too much, too soon you may notice your bleeding increase. This is your body telling you to slow down. Listen to your body and your baby, and don't hesitate to ask if you need extra help. This is your time.

VISITORS

Everyone who comes to visit brings food or pitches in on a household task. It may be a good idea to make a sign to put on the door if it's a bad time for a visit.   Sometimes we schedule visits and then realize in the moment that it isn't the best time. That's okay, simply ask that your visitor leave the meal they are bringing on the doorstep and let them know you'll get ahold of them when everything quiets down. Also, everyone who comes over must wash his or her hands before handling the baby. It's a good idea to make a sign to put up so that everyone who comes into your room is reminded.   If possible, it's also customary to have toddlers and small children to wait to visit until at least two weeks post birth. You will want to keep germs limited in the house, as your new baby is still very susceptible to illness. Use a "chore stick" jar. Write chores on popsicle sticks and put them in a jar; everyone who visits chooses a stick and completes the task.

Making signs to put up around the house can be a fun activity for siblings and helps them feel included.

POSTPARTUM PLAN WORKSHEET

IMPORTANT PHONE NUMBERS

OB/Midwife:

Pediatrician:

Lactation Consultant:

Doula:

Others:

MEALS

Url for food train calendar:

Contact person(s) for meal coordination:

CHORES

List of people who can help out around the house and contact info:

SIBLING AND/OR PET CARE

Contact person for sibling care/play date coordination:

List of people we trust who can provide sibling care and contact info:

FEEDINGS

Planned method of feeding: Breast/chest □   Bottle   □   Both □

Will you be hiring night support from a postpartum doula?
Their contact info:

SLEEP

Planned method of sleeping: Co-sleeping □   Bed sharing   □   Nursery □

ROLES AND DELEGATION

Who will be at home during the day?

Who will be in charge of tidying and housekeeping?

Who will be in charge of alerting friends and family of the birth details? Method used for
alert: Facebook   □   Email blast   □   Voicemail greeting   □

Who will be in charge of night feedings?

Who will be in charge of diaper changes?

How can you find time to be present with each other and maintain intimacy?

Birthing person's expectations of partner in the postpartum period:

Partner's expectations of birthing person in the postpartum period:

CLASSMATE'S CONTACT INFO:

APPENDIXES

APPENDIX A:

ISLAMIC BIRTH TRADITIONS AND CUSTOMS

We are blessed with Allah's gifts of guidance, helping us through the many stages of life. The time of birth, because of its great importance, is rich with rituals that inspire piety and honor the significance of these moments. It is only fitting that every person's first tastes of this world be filled with blessed and wise spiritual acts connecting them to God, their creator, and starting them out on the life long path of devotion to, and love of The Divine.

In births intense moments of unmatched emotional and physical experience we also feel spiritual awakenings that we may never feel the like of in our lives! Our heightened spirituality at the time of birth leads us to performing these rituals with truly heartfelt gratitude and joyous celebration of new life.

It is often difficult for people to differentiate which acts are prescribed by Islamic Sacred Law, and which ones either stem from culture, or a misunderstanding of Islamic Sacred Law. This is why one must consult the opinions of the scholars of one's school of thought, as even within the tradition, there are differences of opinion. Unless specified, the opinions presented here are of the Sunni Majority.

SUMMARY OF RITUALS FOLLOWING BIRTH

Immediately after birth:
The Athan
Tahneek
Naming the Child (or commonly performed on the seventh day)
Rest for 40 days

On the 7th day (or after):
Circumcision
Shaving the Head
Aqiqa

LANDMARK STAGES OF PREGNANCY

Dua of Conception

The Prophet (peace be upon him) said, "If anyone intends to have (sexual intercourse) with his wife, he should say: "Bismillah! Allahumma janibnash-Shaitana, wa jannibish-Shaitana ma razaqtana (In the Name of Allah, O Allah! Keep us away from Satan and keep Satan away from what You have bestowed upon us);' and if Allah has ordained a child for them, Satan will never harm him." (Al-Bukhari and Muslim)

The Baby's Soul Arrives At 120 Days Gestation

Messenger of Allah (peace be upon him), the truthful and the receiver of the truth informed us, saying, "The creation of you (humans) is gathered in the form of semen in the womb of your mother for forty days, then it becomes a clinging thing in similar (period), then it becomes a lump of flesh like that, then Allah sends an angel who breathes the life into it; and (the angel) is commanded to record four things about it: Its provision, its term of life (in this world), its conduct; and whether it will be happy or miserable. By the One besides Whom there is no true god! Verily, one of you would perform the actions of the dwellers of Jannah until there is only one cubit between him and it (Jannah), when what is foreordained would come to pass and he would perform the actions of the inmates of Hell until he enter it. And one of you would perform the actions of the inmates of Hell, until there is only one cubit between him and Hell. Then he would perform the acts of the dwellers of Jannah until he would enter it." (Al- Bukhari and Muslim)

Dua Of Adam And Eve (peace be upon them) In Late Pregnancy

"When it grew heavy they both prayed to Allah their Lord saying: "If You will grant us a healthy child, we will be truly thankful"." (Surah Al-A'raf (#7), Ayah 189)

Find further suggestions for prayers in Appendix B.

GIVE THANKS AND BE CONTENT

When a child is born, the parents and family should give thanks to Allah Most High for the gift He has bestowed on them, and that everything went better than it could have. They should recognize that this baby is a trust from Allah, not something that they own.

They should also be content with Allah Most High's decree regarding the gender and condition of the child, and show their love equally in all cases. They should also announce the birth with the same happiness and thanks to others, and others should congratulate them, also regardless of the gender or other features of the child.

CALLING THE ATHAN IMMEDIATELY AFTER BIRTH

Calling the Athan for the newborn is a sunnah. It should be gently called in the right ear of the child, and the Iqamah should be gently called in the left ear. The wisdom behind it is that the first words the child hears is the magnification of Allah Most High, in hopes that the child would live their life responding to the call to worship their Lord on the path of Islam.

Arabic Text of The Athan:

اللهُ أَكْبَرُ ، اللهُ أَكْبَرُ

اللهُ أَكْبَرُ ، اللهُ أَكْبَرُ

أَشْهَدُ أَنْ لَّا إِلَهَ إِلَّا الله

أَشْهَدُ أَنْ لَّا إِلَهَ إِلَّا الله

أَشْهَدُ أَنَّ مُحَمَّداً رَّسُوْلُ الله

أَشْهَدُ أَنَّ مُحَمَّداً رَّسُوْلُ الله

حَيَّ عَلَى الصَّلَاةِ ، حَيَّ عَلَى الصَّلَاةِ

حَيَّ عَلَى الفَلَاحْ ، حَيَّ عَلَى الفَلَاحْ

اللهُ أَكْبَرُ ، اللهُ أَكْبَرُ

لَا إِلَهَ إِلَّا الله

Transliteration of The Athan:

Allahu Akbar, Allahu Akbar
Allahu Akbar, Allahu Akbar
Ash hadu allaa ilaaha illAllah
Ash hadu allaa ilaaha illAllah
Ash hadu anna Muhammadan rasulullah
Ash hadu anna Muhammadan rasulullah
Hayya a'las salaah, Hayya a'las salaah
Hayya a'lal falaah, Hayya a'lal falaah
Allahu Akbar, Allahu Akbar
La ilaaha illAllah

Arabic Text of The Iqamah:

اللهُ أَكْبَرُ ، اللهُ أَكْبَرُ

أَشْهَدُ أَنْ لَّا إِلَهَ إِلَّا الله

أَشْهَدُ أَنَّ مُحَمَّداً رَّسُوْلُ الله

حَيَّ عَلَى الصَّلَاةِ ، حَيَّ عَلَى الفَلَاحْ

قَدْ قَامَتِ الصَّلَاةُ، قَدْ قَامَتِ الصَّلَاةُ

اللهُ أَكْبَرُ ، اللهُ أَكْبَرُ

لَا إِلَهَ إِلَّا اللهُ

Transliteration of The Iqamah:

Allahu Akbar, Allahu Akbar
Ash hadu allaa ilaaha illAllah
Ash hadu anna Muhammadan rasulullah
Hayya a'las salaah, Hayya a'lal falaah
Qad qaamatis salaah, Qad qaamatis salaah
Allahu Akbar, Allahu Akbar
La ilaaha illAllah

TAHNEEK

It is narrated about the Prophet (peace and blessings be upon him) that when a child was born and brought to him soon afterward, he would chew a small piece of date with his mouth and then place it on the palate of the newborn. It is considered a sunnah act.

This can be done with a date, but if dates are not available, then any similar sweet natural thing that is safe to be given to babies will suffice (honey is not considered safe).

This can be performed by the parent, or upright person in the community, preferably from the people of knowledge and piety. The wisdom is that by sharing the piece of date with a pious Muslim, it is a source of blessing and a hope that the child will also be pious and upright.

NAMING THE CHILD

The naming of the child can be done right away, or one can wait until the seventh day, as some narrations do mention this, however, any time is permissible. It is the child's right that they be given a name that has a good meaning and reflective of the child's Muslim faith.

REST FOR 40 DAYS

The first 40 days postpartum is a time of rest for the mother in most Islamic and Traditional cultures. The mother is experiencing post partum bleeding during this time so exempt from daily prayers and her close family and friends take care of the house work, cooking, and the needs of older children so she and the baby can be fully stress free and focus on recuperation. Rest in the postpartum period improves the future health of the mother, allowing her pelvic floor, internal organs, and ligaments the time to go back to their previous states after undergoing the stresses of pregnancy and birth.This restorative practice preserves her strength and physical integrity for long term health, wellbeing and future childbearing. A reduction in postpartum mood disorders, and better breastfeeding outcomes are also great benefits of this practice.

Despite its deep wisdom and protective nature to the physical and psychological health of the growing family, often times this tradition is the first to be neglected in the hustle and bustle of the modern world.

Consider the care that Allah gave to Maryam directly after she gave birth to Jesus (peace be upon them): "So eat, drink and refresh yourself. If you see anyone, tell him: `I have vowed a fast to Rahman (Allah), so I will not speak to anyone today'." (Surah Maryam (#19), Ayah 26)

146

CIRCUMCISION FOR BOYS

This is removal of a boys foreskin covering the tip of his penis, and is traditionally done on the 7th day after birth, or at a later time in childhood, often in the 7th year of life. Many people disagree with circumcision based largely on the insensitive methods that are commonly employed. Practitioners differ in their methods, and commitment to reducing the discomfort that the child experiences during this procedure. You may need to ask around and weigh your options. A practitioner that does house calls, such as a Jewish Mohel, may be an option,.

In the Hanafi and Maliki schools, circumcision is an emphasized sunnah for boys, as it is amongst the signs of Islam and an act of natural disposition (fitra). In the Shafi'i and Hanbali schools, it is considered obligatory. Cleanliness for prayer is a major reason for its importance.

SHAVING THE HEAD

Shaving the head is recommended for boys and girls both, on the seventh day. The shaved hair is then weighed, and its weight in silver or gold is given away in charity, while the hair is then buried (as we would do with any part of the human body that is separated from it like hair, nails, and the placenta). This is done out of thanks for being blessed with the baby by showing servitude to Allah through sacrificing the hair, and invoking Allah's blessings through giving in charity.

AQIQAH

The aqiqah is recommended, and optimally performed on the seventh day. It is when an animal is ritually sacrificed out of gratitude for being blessed with the newborn, and often, people are fed. This can be combined with the shaving of the head and naming, or not.

THE ROLE OF CULTURE AND FAMILY CUSTOMS

In some cultures, the recommended and sunnah acts that we mentioned have become wrongly seen as almost obligatory, even if the parents cannot afford it, and it can also reflect elements of trying to impress society, or ward off superstitions.

If an act is obligatory, it must not be downplayed or ignored, and on the other hand, if an act is recommended or sunnah, it is good to follow if one wishes, but it should not be over-emphasized until it becomes a pressure on the parents of the newborn, or overexerts the frail physical and emotional states of the mother and baby.

The point behind all of these rituals, is that they should come from a grateful heart, one that is aware of the immense blessing of parenthood, and the sacred duty of a parent to its child.

If you do not to perform the recommended rituals completely there is no harm in doing any part of the rituals that you can do, delaying them, or leaving them unperformed. Performing Cultural practices that do not go against Islamic principles are fine, such as having a baby shower, but should not replace the Islamic rituals.

RAISING PIOUS CHILDREN

Moving forward in your lives as parents you may find benefit from an excellent article by Hina Khan-Mukhtar about raising pious children called,"Raising Children With Deen And Dunya".

May Allah Most High bless your child and make them amongst the pious and righteous!

APPENDIX B:

PRAYERS DURING LABOR

QURAN

Surah Al Fatihah (#1): It is effective to read for any purpose, and especially benefits situations where opening is desired.

Surah Maryam (#19): Commonly read during pregnancy and birth.

> Note: Ayahs 16-36 describe the story of the immaculate conception, birth, and soon after it. Many women find it inspiring and comforting to read.

> Links to a film called Maryam al Muqaddasa:
> This is an excellent Iranian film originally in Persian
> Dubbed over in English: https://www.youtube.com/watch?v=0Wjz1z4oEls
> English subtitles: https://www.youtube.com/watch?v=_9XWDMewYbM

Surah Al-Anbiyaa (#21), Ayah 87:
The prayer of Prophet Yunus (Jonah) (peace be upon him) while trapped in the belly of the whale:

Arabic text: لَا إِلَهَ إِلَّا أَنْتَ سُبْحَانَكَ إِنِّي كُنْتُ مِنَ الظَّالِمِينَ

Transliteration: "La ilaaha illa Anta Subhanaka innee kuntu minaz zhalimeen"
Translation: "There is no god but You, glory be to You! Indeed I was the one who committed wrong."

Surah Yasin (#36): It is effective to read for any purpose.

Surah Dukhan (#44)

Surah al-Fath' (#48), Ayah 1:
إِنَّا فَتَحْنَا لَكَ فَتْحًا مُبِينًا
"Surely We have granted you a manifest victory"

Surah Abasa (#80), Ayah 20:

Arabic text: ثُمَّ السَّبِيلَ يَسَّرَهُ

Transliteration: "Thummas sabeela yassarah"
Translation: "then makes his way of life smooth for him"

Surah Inshirah (#94)

AMULETS (TALISMANS)

Surah Dukhan (#44): (wise to reserve for difficult labors only): To be written in Arabic (no dots or voweling necessary) on a piece of paper, folded up, covered in something that no smells can penetrate (so that one can wear it in the bathroom without disrespecting it), and worn on the body while in labor.

Surah Yunus (#10), Ayah 32
To be written on the peel of a sweet squash and bound to the woman's arm.

فَذَٰلِكُمُ اللَّهُ رَبُّكُمُ الْحَقُّ ۖ فَمَاذَا بَعْدَ الْحَقِّ إِلَّا الضَّلَالُ ۖ فَأَنَّىٰ تُصْرَفُونَ

The same Allah is your real Lord: What is left after the truth except falsehood? How then can you turn away?

From Tibb an-Nabawi (Medicine of the Prophet):
To be written in Arabic (no dots or voweling necessary) on the inside of a clean vessel in edible ink (like saffron water), then filled with water and the pregnant woman drinks from it and it is sprinkled on her abdomen.

1.

لَا إِلَهَ إِلَّا اللهُ، الرَّؤُوفُ الرَّحِيْمِ، الحَمْدُ لله رَبِّ العَرْشِ العَظِيمِ

There is no god but God, the Clement the Gracious; praise be to God the Lord of the mighty Throne.

Surah Al-Fatiha (#1), Ayah 2
الْحَمْدُ لله رَبِّ الْعَالَمِينَ
All praise is for Allah, the Lord of the Worlds

Surah An-Nazi'at (#79), Ayah 46

كَأَنَّهُمْ يَوْمَ يَرَوْنَهَا لَمْ يَلْبَثُوا إِلَّا عَشِيَّةً أَوْ ضُحَاهَا

On that Day when they shall see it, they shall feel as if they had stayed in this world only one evening or one morning.

Surah Al-Ahqaf (#46), Ayah 35

كَأَنَّهُمْ يَوْمَ يَرَوْنَ مَا يُوعَدُونَ لَمْ يَلْبَثُوا إِلَّا سَاعَةً مِنْ نَهَارٍ ۚ بَلَاغٌ ۚ فَهَلْ يُهْلَكُ إِلَّا الْقَوْمُ الْفَاسِقُونَ

On the Day when they shall see that which they are being threatened with, their life on earth will seem to them as if they had lived no more than an hour of a day. The Message of forewarning has been conveyed. Shall any be destroyed except the transgressors?

2.

Surah Al-Inshiqaq (#84), Ayaat 1-4

إِذَا السَّمَاءُ انْشَقَّتْ
وَأَذِنَتْ لِرَبِّهَا وَحُقَّتْ
وَإِذَا الْأَرْضُ مُدَّتْ
وَأَلْقَتْ مَا فِيهَا وَتَخَلَّتْ

When heaven will split asunder,
obeying her Lord's command as she ought to.
When the earth will spread out
and cast out all that is within her and becomes empty

From Imam Al Ghazali:

This is made up of Arabic numbers (top), and letters (bottom), and is meant to be worn in the arch of the left foot during labor for ease

٤ ذ	٩ ط	٢ ب
٣ ج	٥ ه	٧ ز
٨ ح	١ أ	٦ و

NAMES OF ALLAH

May be used in a variety of ways. Commonly they are repeated silently or out loud as a supplication during labor.

Ya Rahman (يَا رَحْمٰن): Oh Most Gracious

Ya Raheem (يَا رَحِيم): Oh Most Merciful

Ya Salaam (يَا سَلام): Oh Source of Peace

Ya Fattaah (يَا فَتَّاح): Oh Opener of All Portals, Oh Giver of Victory

Ya Baasit (يَا بَاسِط): Oh Expander

Ya Lateef (يَا لَطِيف): Oh Most Kind (**this name is used often**)

Ya Kareem (يَا كَرِيم): Oh Most Generous

Ya Mujeeb (يَا مُجِيب): Oh Most Expedient Answerer

Ya Wadud (يَا وَدُود): Oh Most Loving and Kind

Ya Wali (يَا وَلِيّ): Oh Best Protecting Friend

Ya Muhyi (يَا مُحْيِي): Oh Giver of Life

Ya Ra'uf (يَا رَؤُوف): Oh Most Compassionate

Ya Khaliq (يَا خَالِق): Oh Creator

Ya Nafi' (يَا نَافِع): Oh Bestower of Benefits

Ya Noor (يَا نُور): Oh Prime Light

SALAWAAT

Sending Peace and Blessings on the Prophet Muhammad is always a powerfully calming prayer. It has been found to be very effective during labor.

"The Messenger of Allah (peace be upon him) came one day with a joyful expression on his face. He said: "Jibril came to me and said: 'Will it not please you, O Muhammad, (to know) that no one of your Ummah will send salah upon you but I will send salah upon him tenfold, and no one will send salams upon you but I will send salams upon him tenfold?" "   (Sunan an-Nasa'i)

Here is one form of many:
السَّلَامُ عَلَيْكَ أَيُّهَا النَّبِيُّ وَرَحْمَةُ الله وَ بَرَكَاتُه
As salaam Alaika ayuhan nabiyyu wa rahmatullahi wa barakatuh
Peace be upon you Oh Prophet and the mercy of Allah and His blessings

PERFORMING OBLIGATORY PRAYERS IN LABOR

It continues to be obligatory to pray the 5 daily prayers throughout labor, until the birth of the baby. If you are unable to pray one of the 5 daily prayers during labor, it should be made up after the period of postpartum bleeding, when you resume praying. The natural hormones of labor usually effect brain function and take a woman out of her thinking brain. Because of this many women find that prayer is not possible in active labor. Allah knows your intention, and that is what matters in this and other similar situations.

For more information, please reference "Prayer and Labor and Delivery",
a thorough article on this topic by Anse Tamara Grey found at: www.muslimobgyn.com

THE FLOWER OF MARYAM

The Flower of Maryam (*Anastatica hierochuntica*) is a small shrub collected across North Africa, Saudi Arabia, Iran, and Pakistan, and among other applications it is used to bring pain relief and support for childbirth. The dried plant is placed in a bowl of warm water during labor and as labor progresses and the plant rehydrates, uncurling and expanding, the laboring woman sips from the water. Whether its medicinal properties encourage dilation, or if it's a powerful visualization tool for mothers, traditional midwives have used the Flower of Maryam with their laboring mothers for hundreds of years.

NOTES:

If you are not accustomed to using the prayers you are inclined towards using during labor, it is a good idea to practice reciting them before labor begins.

Plan on using what ever prayers feel right to you in the moment, and don't worry if nothing feels right to you. A heart that is centered on God doesn't need words. God is all knowing and all seeing, his assistance is not dependent on particular words! There is a famous poem sung by the Yemenis that beautifully expresses this truth:

قَدْ كَفَانِي عِلْمُ رَبِّي مِنْ سُؤَالِي وَ اخْتِيَارِي

My Lord's knowledge has sufficed me from asking or choosing

APPENDIX C:
ORIGINAL RELAXATIONS

1. SCENT/SMELL RELAXATION

Choose a scent that has qualities that you need right now.
Put the scent close to you so that you can smell it, but don't need to be holding it. You can use an essential oil diffuser, scented candle, incense, or simply put a container with a scent nearby. **Make sure it is not so strong that it will bother you during the relaxation.*
Get absolutely comfortable in either a sitting or lying position, being supported completely by pillows. Turn off the ringer on your phone and make sure that you are not hungry, thirsty, or needing to use the restroom so that you can be free to fall into a deep relaxing state with no interruptions. *If you plan to use aromatherapy in labor, please see our handout on best practices on page 38.*

The practice:

Start with 3 deep diaphragmatic (aka belly) breaths. Breathe in through the nose, feeling your belly rise. Breathe out, emptying all the air in your lungs by pulling your bellybutton toward your spine. The speed of your breathing is slow, relaxed, natural and comfortable.

With each out breath release tension in your body. Surrender, and sink into the pillows or wherever you lie.

- Take a deep breath in, breathe out and release your head, neck and, shoulders.

- Take a deep breath in, breathe out and release your chest, mid back, torso and belly.

- Take a deep breath in, breathe out and release your legs, hips, ankles, and feet.

Now turn your attention to the scent and allow yourself to fully experience it: Notice everything: your body, your thoughts, your memories. Let your mind and body be fully in the experience of this wonderful aroma and all it has to offer you. Stay with the scent and this feeling of relaxation as an integrated experience. Let your thoughts just float by while you breathe and enjoy for as long as is comfortable.

2. BREATH RELAXATION

Get absolutely comfortable in either a sitting or lying position, being supported completely by pillows. Turn off the ringer on your phone and make sure that you are not hungry, thirsty, or needing to use the restroom so that you can be free to fall into a deep relaxing state with no interruptions. It is ok if you fall asleep. You need as much rest as you can get; consider it a bonus if you get to catch a nap!

Have a partner or friend read this script to you. As they read, have them pause for a minute in between each statement. When the reader gets to the end of the script, they can quietly sneak out and leave you to continue your relaxation until you are ready to come out of it. If you would prefer to do this practice on your own, simply record yourself reading the script and play it back once you are nice and comfortable.

The practice:

Start with 3 deep diaphragmatic (aka belly) breaths. Breathe in through your nose, feeling your belly rise. Breathe out slowly, emptying all of the air in your lungs by pulling your bellybutton toward your spine. The speed of your breathing is slow, relaxed, natural and comfortable. With each breath out, release tension in your body, surrender, and sink deeper into the pillows or where you lie.

- Take a deep breath in, breathe out and release your head, neck, shoulders, arms, and hands.

- Take a deep breath in, breathe out and release your chest, mid back, torso and belly.

- Take a deep breath in, breathe out and release your legs, hips, ankles and feet.

Close your eyes.
Imagine you are at the seaside. It is beautiful and the waves are coming and going in a natural rhythm. The sea air smells wonderful.
You instinctively want to take long deep breaths of the lovely sea air into your lungs. The misty air fills your lungs and circulates through your body, oxygenating all of your cells.
You find that in order to get a fulfilling breath, you must breath from your diaphragm. You feel your lungs, and belly expand with each breath in. Breathing out feels just as good. You feel that your cells are being cleansed as you deeply release and let go of the used up air.
Breathe in and oxygenate you and your baby, breathe out and release anywhere that there is tension in your body. (say this three times)
Stay at the ocean as long as you are comfortable.

155

3. BODY AWARENESS RELAXATION

Through tensing and then relaxing each part of the body, you will identify areas that hold the most tension and learn how to efficiently release them. In labor, holding tension and gripping or tightening any muscle group can have a negative effect of prompting the fear, tension, pain cycle. The most common areas that tension is held in labor are the jaw, shoulders, hands, abdomen, hips, and buttocks. This tension wastes valuable energy and may prevent labor's progress. Conversely, relaxation of your muscles reduces your heart rate and blood pressure, as well as decreases your respiration rates. Relaxation is also an excellent tool to conserve energy for the duration of your labor. Remember: after first stage labor, you'll still have the pushing phase and will want to be as rested as possible in preparation.

The practice:

Get absolutely comfortable in either a sitting or lying position, being supported completely by pillows. Turn off the ringer on your phone and make sure that you are not hungry, thirsty, or needing to use the restroom so that you can be free to fall into a deep relaxing state with no interruptions.

Have a partner or friend read this script to you. As they read, have them pause for a few seconds in between each statement. When the reader gets to the end of the script, they can quietly sneak out and leave you to continue your relaxation until you are ready to come out of it. If you would prefer to do this practice on your own, simply record yourself reading the script and play it back once you are nice and comfortable.

Start with 3 deep diaphragmatic (aka belly) breaths. Breathe in through your nose, feeling your belly rise. Breathe out slowly, emptying all of the air in your lungs by pulling your bellybutton toward your spine. The speed of your breathing is slow, relaxed, natural and comfortable. With each breath out, release tension in your body, surrender, and sink deeper into the pillows or where you lie.

- Take a deep breath in, breathe out and release your head, neck, shoulders, arms, and hands.

- Take a deep breath in, breathe out and release your chest, mid back, torso and belly.

- Take a deep breath in, breathe out and release your legs, hips, ankles and feet.

During this relaxation I will ask you to tense various muscles throughout your body. Please do this without straining. You do not need to exert yourself, just contract each muscle firmly but gently as you breathe in. If you feel uncomfortable at any time, you can simply relax and breathe normally.

Bring your awareness to your feet and toes. Breathe in deeply through your nose, and as you do, gently flex your feet upward toward your shin. Hold your breath for just a few seconds and then release the muscles in your feet as you breathe out. Feel the tension in your feet wash away as you exhale. Notice how different your feet feel when tensed and when they are relaxed. Feel yourself relaxing more and more deeply with each breath. Your whole body is becoming heavier, softer, and more relaxed as each moment passes.

Draw in a deep breath and tighten your leg muscles. Hold for a few seconds, and then let it all go as you breathe out. Feel your muscles relax, and the tension washing away with your out-breath.

Take another breath and this time and gradually tighten all the muscles in your legs, from your feet to your buttocks. Do this in whatever way feels natural and comfortable to you. Hold it - and now release all these large strong muscles as you breathe out. Enjoy the sensation of release as you become even more deeply relaxed.

Now bring your awareness to your abdomen. Draw in a nice, deep breath tightening these muscles. Imagine you are trying to touch your belly button to your spine. Now release your breath and let all of these abdominal muscles relax. Notice the sensation of relief that comes from letting go. Once again, draw in a deep breath, tightening your abdominal muscles. Hold for a few seconds, and then let them relax completely as you exhale and release all tension.

Now bring your awareness to the muscles in your back. As you slowly breathe in, arch your back slightly and tighten these muscles. Release your breath and let your back muscles relax completely. Again, draw in a deep breath, tightening your back muscles. Hold for the count of three, and then let them relax and release completely.

Now take your attention to your shoulder and neck muscles. As you slowly draw in a nice, deep breath, pull your shoulders up toward your ears tightening them firmly. Breathe out completely and allow the contracted neck and shoulder muscles to go loose and limp, fully relaxed.

Once more, pull your shoulders up toward your ears and tighten their muscles firmly. Let our your breath and feel the tension subside as you relax and breathe out. Feel the heaviness in your body now, enjoying the relaxation. Feel yourself becoming heavier and heavier. Feel yourself becoming more and more deeply relaxed. You are calm, secure, and at peace.

Now it's time to let go of all the tension in your arms and hands. Start with your upper arms. As you breathe in, raise your wrists towards your shoulders and tighten the muscles in your upper arms. Hold that breath and that contraction for just a moment, and then gently lower your arms and breathe all the way out. You may feel a warm, burning sensation in your muscles when you tighten them. Feel how relaxing it is to release that tightness and to breathe away all tension. Your arms are completely limp.

As you curl your upper arms again, tighten the muscles as you breathe in. Breathe in deeply. As you breathe out, relax your arms completely, even more than the time before.

Now bring your awareness to your forearms. As you breathe in, curl your hands inwards as though you are trying to touch the inside of your elbows with your fingertips. As you breathe out, feel the tension subside as your forearms relax and release.

Again, take a deep breath in, tightening the muscles in your forearms. Hold it for a moment, and then release. Feel the tension washing away completely. Your arms are fully relaxed.

157

Take a breath in and tightly clench your fists. When you have finished breathing in, hold for the count of three, and then release your hands. Your hands are so soft and relaxed. Take another deep breath in, clenching your fists. Hold for the count of three and then release your hands once more. Let your fingers go limp. Your arms and hands are feeling so heavy and relaxed. Take a couple of nice long slow breaths now, and just relax completely. Feel yourself slipping even deeper into a state of complete rest.

Tighten the muscles in your face by squeezing your eyes shut and clenching your lips together as you take a deep breath in. Hold it for the count of three, then breathe out and relax all your facial muscles. Feel your face softening completely, your tongue loose in your mouth. Once more, breathe in deeply while you tighten the muscles in your eyes and lips. And release.

Bring your awareness to the muscles in your jaw. Take a deep breath in, opening your mouth as wide as you can. Feel your jaw muscles stretching and tightening as your mouth opens. Exhale and let your jaw go slack, feeling your tongue limp and loose in your mouth. Breathe into your jaw and release any tension that still remains. Again, fill your lungs with air, opening your mouth wide. Breathe out and let your mouth relax completely. Let your breath flow all the way out of your lungs.

You are now completely relaxed from the tips of your toes to the top of your head. Enjoy this feeling and take a few more minutes to rest.

Relax. Listen to the sound of your breathing and enjoy the lovely, warm sensation of full, pure physical relaxation. If you have the time, feel free to fall asleep. You will wake feeling completely rejuvenated, relaxed, and energized.

4. TOUCH RELAXATION

This relaxation exercise is designed to be practiced with your partner, doula, or a loved one: anyone that you trust who will be an active participant at your birth. The benefits of practicing this relaxation together (we suggest a minimum of once a week):

Touch is bonding. Get your oxytocin and feel good love hormones flowing. Oxytocin is released when we are with people who we love and that care for us in a loving way. Oxytocin is released with loving touch. The baby also reaps benefits whenever his/her birthing parent gets a burst of oxytocin; this oxytocin 'bath' sends a message to the baby that life is safe, and feels good!

With practice, your partner will be more confident in these techniques, so practice them often. The more confident he/she/they are, the more solidly supported you feel and the easier it is to let yourself go deeper into labor's altered state of consciousness. In this space, you can find your focus and rhythm knowing that your labor support is focused on you, your work, and relaxation. Furthermore, when your partner/s and helper/s feel confident in these techniques, they can feel the joy of the birth process, rather than fear and doubt in themselves.

Throughout this course we will be teaching you a variety of touch, pressure, and massage techniques. Labor is a fluid and continually changing process and you will not know what it is that feels relieving or good in labor until you are experiencing it. Your touch preferences can change as quickly as your labor in flow and intensity, so having as many tools ready in your "toolbox" as possible puts you at a great advantage in preparation for your birth experience. Before beginning this practice, make sure your partner is wearing comfortable clothes and has at least 15-20 minutes to focus on this exercise without feeling rushed or needed elsewhere.

Find some music that is relaxing for the both of you.

When you are through with this relaxation practice, take time to discuss what you liked and what you did not like; which areas that you would have liked your partner to focus on longer and areas that you don't like to be touched. Be sure to also show your partner how you would like him/her/them to adjust so that their touch works best for you.

Get absolutely comfortable in either a sitting or lying position, being supported completely by pillows. Turn off the ringer on your phone and make sure that you are not hungry, thirsty, or needing to use the restroom so that you can be free to fall into a deep relaxing state with no interruptions. Put on the music, making sure it isn't too loud. As you relax, the music will appear louder, so it's best to start at a lower volume so that it remains relaxing throughout the exercise.

***Partners, be aware that this will be a meditative exercise for you as well. Get comfortable and remember to stay present.
Sit in a comfortable position and do the 3 breaths together. This will bring you into your body and prepare you to be present and relaxed.

The practice:

Start with 3 deep diaphragmatic (aka belly) breaths. Breathe in through your nose, feeling your belly rise. Breathe out slowly, emptying all of the air in your lungs by pulling your bellybutton toward your spine. The speed of your breathing is slow, relaxed, natural and comfortable. With each breath out, release tension in your body, surrender, and sink deeper into the pillows or where you lie.

- Take a deep breath in, breathe out and release your head, neck, shoulders, arms, and hands.

- Take a deep breath in, breathe out and release your chest, mid back, torso and belly.

- Take a deep breath in, breathe out and release your legs, hips, ankles and feet.

Take a moment to notice how your body feels. There will be parts that are more relaxed and free of tension than others. Don't try to change anything right now; just notice any discomfort, tight muscles, aches, and pains.

Partners: start with the head, working your way slowly down the body, ending at the feet. Hold a relaxing pressure to each part of her/his/their body with intention and love. Breathe slow diaphragmatic breaths, in for 4 out for 4 and feel the response in your partner's body with each hand/pressure placement. You will use your intuition to guide you in how long to stay with each part of the body and this will be a very good practice for intuitive touch during labor and birth.

Pregnant partners, it is your job to breathe into the areas you are being touched: in for 4 and out for 4 with every placement of your partner's hands. Bring breath in, and release tension with the out breath. Partners end this practice holding the feet with firm, steady pressure until you both feel complete.

5. SOUND RELAXATION

This relaxation exercise will combine relaxing music with a guided visualization. We recommend the music you choose to be calming and instrumental so that it doesn't take your focus from your visualization. Through practice, your brain will automatically start filling you with light and relaxation when you hear music. The more you practice this script, the more automatic relaxation will come to you when you put it into practice. This is a simple concept that is used in many meditation practices around the world. As with any pre-written visualizations, we encourage you to replace any language or word use that doesn't flow easily for you; replacing with your own version.

Get absolutely comfortable in either a sitting or lying position, being supported completely by pillows. Turn off the ringer on your phone and make sure that you are not hungry, thirsty, or needing to use the restroom so that you can be free to fall into a deep relaxing state with no interruptions.

Have a partner or friend read this script to you. As they read, have them pause for one minute in between each statement. When the reader gets to the end of the script, they can quietly sneak out and leave you to continue your relaxation until you are ready to come out of it. If you would prefer to do this practice on your own, simply record yourself reading this script and play it back once you are nice and comfortable. **After a couple of practices, it will be easy to pull this visualization scene up in your mind without any help. This is precisely why we recommend you practice relaxation and visualization often in preparation for childbirth, so that your body can find a place of deep relaxation without any effort while you do the work of bringing your baby into this world.**

The practice:

Start with 3 deep diaphragmatic (aka belly) breaths. Breathe in through your nose, feeling your belly rise. Breathe out slowly, emptying all of the air in your lungs by pulling your bellybutton toward your spine. The speed of your breathing is slow, relaxed, natural and comfortable. With each breath out, release tension in your body, surrender, and sink deeper into the pillows or where you lie.

- Take a deep breath in, breathe out and release your head, neck, shoulders, arms, and hands.

- Take a deep breath in, breathe out and release your chest, mid back, torso and belly.

- Take a deep breath in, breathe out and release your legs, hips, ankles and feet.

Imagine you are in a room. This room is the embodiment of comfort and safety. The room has the perfect temperature and lighting, and your favorite relaxing music is playing. You are so comfortable and relaxed right where you are. Picture your perfect comfy bed, chair, hammock, etc. that you are in.

The room is all yours, and no one is allowed to knock or come in until you want company, so know that you will not be interrupted. This is your time.

Imagine a brilliant, white light above your head. Picture this light as a beam, coming down onto the top of your head and radiating into it. As you breathe, envision that light slowly filling your body, starting with your head, and down into your face, neck and shoulders. The brilliant, warm, white light travels down your body, filling every single cell as it moves. Each breath brings more light into your body. This light is life affirming and calming, filling you with a sense of wellbeing and safety. All is well and as it should be. Each breath you take brings oxygen filled with this calming, loving light to you and your baby.

Imagine the light traveling down your arms to your fingertips. It fills your torso. See your uterus and baby filling up with this light and you both feel nothing but calm, relaxation, and love. The light now fills your lower body and legs.

Light continues to fill your body, ankles, feet and toes.

The light now fills your whole body, your whole being. It overflows and travels out the bottom of your feet and the top of your head. It flows out the sides of your body and your hands. It expands to surround your whole body, enclosing you and the baby in its purity, love, and protection. You are completely relaxed and feel trust, love, and safety.

Keep breathing and hold the image of this light for as long as is needed. When you are complete, you can slowly come out of your relaxation, feeling energized and peaceful.

6. VOICE RELAXATION

Our breath is one of the most effective relaxation tools that we possess. All relaxation and meditation techniques have breath in common. Breathing is automatic; we go through the day without thinking about it. We do however, from time to time feel stressed, and in this state tend to take shallower shorter breaths, not fully exhaling. Most of us have a built-in response to these moments that makes us take deep breaths to calm ourselves in stressful situations. Our bodies know that it is difficult to be stressed or panicked when we are taking deep, slow breaths, filling our lungs with oxygen, and slowly releasing until our lungs are completely empty.

Deep breathing:

- Calms the nervous system

- Releases good feeling neuro-chemicals in the brain

- Relaxes the muscles

- Lowers blood pressure

- Activates our parasympathetic nervous system, or "rest and digest" (benefits our digestive system)

Before we begin...

Get absolutely comfortable in either a sitting or lying position, being supported completely by pillows. Turn off the ringer on your phone and make sure that you are not hungry, thirsty, or needing to use the restroom so that you can be free to fall into a deep relaxing state with no interruptions.
Have a partner or friend read this script to you. As they read, have them pause for one minute in between each statement. When the reader gets to the end of the script, they can quietly sneak out and leave you to continue your relaxation until you are ready to come out of it. If you would prefer to do this practice on your own, simply record yourself reading the script and play it back once you are nice and comfortable.

The practice:

Start with 3 deep diaphragmatic (aka belly) breaths. Breathe in through your nose, feeling your belly rise. Breathe out slowly, emptying all of the air in your lungs by pulling your bellybutton toward your spine. The speed of your breathing is slow, relaxed, natural and comfortable.
With each breath out, release tension in your body, surrender, and sink deeper into the pillows or where you lie.

- Take a deep breath in, breathe out and release your head, neck, shoulders, arms, and hands.

- Take a deep breath in, breathe out and release your chest, mid back, torso and belly.

- Take a deep breath in, breathe out and release your legs, hips, ankles and feet.

Now that you are relaxed and your nervous system begun to calm itself, bring your awareness to your breathing. is it shallow, fast, slow, or deep? Do a quick scan of your body, noticing any areas that are tense or sore. How does your stomach feel? Are you stressed about anything from the day?

Now take a controlled, full breath in through your nose until your lungs are completely full of air. Breathe from the diaphragm. You will feel your belly rise. Notice how refreshing it is to get a full deep breath in. Exhale through your mouth slowly, until your lungs have completely emptied.

Repeat: Inhale in through your nose slowly, relaxing the diaphragm to make room for your lungs to expand and fill with oxygen. Again: Exhale through your mouth slowly, until your lungs have completely emptied.

Let your body decide when to take the next deep diaphragmatic breath and when to exhale.

Keep breathing in, and out slowly and completely. While you are breathing, do another complete body scan, from head to toe. Are the tense areas softening? Focus on releasing any tension you find with your exhalation.

SCAN YOUR BODY

- The top of your head

- Forehead

- Jaw

- Neck

- Shoulders

- Chest

- Arms and hands

- Torso

- Belly

- Back

- Low back

- Hips & buttocks

- Thighs

- Knees

- Calves

- Ankles

- Feet & toes

Now feel how your body and mind have responded to relaxation. Stay in this deep, restful, calm, and oxygenated state as long as feels comfortable.

Use this breathing technique any time, anywhere. Try practicing taking these breaths a couple times once per hour throughout the day to make sure that you are as relaxed as possible.

7. SIGHT RELAXATION

Today you will explore your relationship with color, by using diaphragmatic breathing and visualization. Every culture has their own relationship to color. Color has it's own energy. Colors are simply waves vibrating at different frequencies. Color has the ability to elicit a range of emotions: calm, excitement, annoyance. It may bring up anger, spark memories, put us in a daydream state, make us hungry, as well as countless other responses.

You may subconsciously or even consciously choose the colors of your wardrobe and what you wear on a daily basis. One day you will want to wear the red shirt. It looks fantastic; it makes you happy. The next day, when you put on the same shirt it just doesn't look or feel right. You choose to put on a different color shirt, and it feels 'right'. You needed vibrancy and energy yesterday, when today you need grounding and confidence.

Breathing in color can have the very same effect as vocalizing and touch. It can activate the gate control response, closing our nervous system's gates to pain messages. You may already have a foundation in the study of the Chakra system. Chakras are said to be energy centers in our body. Each energy center has a different color associated with it, and it's own energetics. If you have previous experience or an affinity for Chakra work, you may find yourself automatically utilizing the color system of the chakras in this exercise.

Get absolutely comfortable in either a sitting or lying position, being supported completely by pillows. Turn off the ringer on your phone and make sure that you are not hungry, thirsty, or needing to use the restroom so that you can be free to fall into a deep relaxing state with no interruptions.

Have a partner or friend read this script to you. As they read, have them pause for a few seconds between each statement. When the reader gets to the end of the script, they can quietly sneak out and leave you to continue your relaxation until you are ready to come out of it. If you would prefer to do this practice on your own, simply record yourself reading the script and play it back once you are nice and comfortable.

The practice:

Start with 3 deep diaphragmatic (aka belly) breaths. Breathe in through your nose, feeling your belly rise. Breathe out slowly, emptying all of the air in your lungs by pulling your bellybutton toward your spine. The speed of your breathing is slow, relaxed, natural and comfortable. With each breath out, release tension in your body, surrender, and sink deeper into the pillows or where you lie.

- Take a deep breath in, breathe out and release your head, neck, shoulders, arms, and hands.

- Take a deep breath in, breathe out and release your chest, mid back, torso and belly.

- Take a deep breath in, breathe out and release your legs, hips, ankles and feet.

Choose a color that resonates with you today. Imagine this color as a mist filling the room. This mist comes down into the top of your head as you breathe. See and feel the color filling your body slowly, starting with your head, face, neck and shoulders. The color mist travels down your body, filling up every single cell.

Each breath brings you more color. This color is life affirming and calming. It fills you with a sense of wellbeing and safety. All is well and as it should be. Each breath brings oxygen filled with this color to you and your baby.

Imagine the colored mist traveling down your arms to your fingertips. It is filling your torso.

See your uterus and baby filling up with this color, filling you with calm, trust, and love. The colored mist now fills your lower body and legs. Colored mist continues to fill your body, moving down your ankles, feet, and toes. The colored mist is now filling your whole body, your whole being. It overflows out the bottom of your feet and the top of your head. It flows out the sides of your body and your hands. It expands to surround your whole body; enclosing you and the baby in pure color, love, trust, and protection.

Keep breathing and hold the image of the color for as long as you need. When you are complete, you can slowly come out of your relaxation, feeling energized and peaceful.

GLOSSARY OF ISLAMIC TERMS

Alhamdulillah: All praise is due to God.

Allah: God, The ever existent and singular, creator and sustainer of all things.

Athan: Call to prayer.

Bismillah: In the name of God.

Cleanliness for prayer: Taharah. Cleanliness of the body, clothing, and place of prayer that is required as a condition to correctly performing an obligatory prayer.

Deen: Way of life.

Dua: Supplication, Prayer.

Emphasized Sunnah: Sunnah Muakkadah. An Act that was performed by the Prophet (peace be upon him) on a regular basis and rarely left unperformed.

Fard: Obligatory.

Hadith: A saying, act, or response, usually of the Prophet Muhammad (peace be upon him).

InshaAllah: If God wills.

Iqamah: Call to signify the start of a prayer.

Islam: Religion of the Muslims.

Islamic: Being in accordance with the religion of Islam.

Islamic Sacred Law: Sharia. Rules that are mainly derived from Quran and Hadith.

MashaAllah: It is what God wills.

Messenger: A Prophet of God who was ordered to teach his people the message of Islam.

Muhammad: The last Prophet of God. He was sent to deliver the message of Islam to all of humanity.

Muslim: A follower of the religion of Islam.

Mustahabb: Recommended, liked.

Obligatory: Fard, a compulsory act according to Islamic law.

Peace be upon him: We state this phrase every time a Prophet's name is mentioned because it is an Islamically recommended practice and an expression of gratitude for all they have done for humanity.

Prophet: A man chosen by God to receive the divine message of true belief.

Quran: The words of God in the form of a holy book revealed to The Prophet Muhammad (peace be upon him). It is the holy scripture of Islam.

Recommended: Mustahabb, liked.

Salawaat: Any words that invoke peace upon The Prophet Muhammad (peace be upon him).

School of Thought: Mathhab.

Sunnah: Actions that were performed or approved of by The Prophet Muhammad (peace be upon him).

Sunni: The largest denomination of Islam.

Tayammum: Dry ablution. Performed in the absence of water or when one is unable to use water. Performed by making an intention, then wiping the face and forearms with a natural substance of the ground/earth.

Thikr: Remembrance of God.

Wudu: Ritual purity. Performed by making an intention, then with water rinsing the face, rinsing the forearms, wiping the head, and rinsing the feet.

The Cornerstone Method of Childbirth Education

Engage. Inform. Empower.

ACKNOWLEDGMENTS

First, Nickie and Juli would like to acknowledge all of the doulas, midwives, childbirth educators, parents, babies, and children of the world who are working to create a more gentle, loving, and peaceful place for us all to live. By bringing in more love, respect, and empowerment to the birth experience, you are doing a huge part to create peace on this planet. We thank you from the bottom of our hearts.

We would like to thank everyone who came together to help create this manual. Without your input, support, and immense creativity, we would not have been able to pull this off.

THE MUSLIM EDITION CO-AUTHOR:
Nethal Abdul-Mu'min - student midwife, childbirth educator, doula, BA in Arabic and Islamic Studies from Abi Nour University in Damascus, Syria, and Quran teacher at Zaytuna College
www.soulfulpassage.com
www.soulfulrecitation.com

PHOTOGRAPHY:
Sophia Harris – student midwife, doula, and photographer
www.sophiadoula.com
Walter M. Ford – doula, childbirth educator, and photographer
www.waltermford.com
Aaliyah Tatum - student midwife, and photographer
A.T (@rebellious.photography) Instagram photos and videos

ILLUSTRATORS:
Beca Irizzary
Maryam Masud, a student at Zaytuna College
www.maryammasud.com

MODELS:
Wren Songbird
Aziza Cree
Baby Songbird/Cree
Jen Loy
Ross Kennedy
Baby boy Loy/Kennedy
Walter M. Ford
Scott Doolin
Shannon Costa
Baby Noah Doolin
Nethal Abdul-Mu'min

ON-LOCATION PHOTO SHOOTS:
San Francisco Birth Center
Midwives Nancy Myrick, Sara Van Acker, and Julie Birdsong
2300 Sutter St. #301
San Francisco, Ca 94115
www.sfbirthcenter.com

Awaken Chiropractic
3515 Grand Ave.
Oakland, CA 94610
www.awakenoakland.com

COVER DESIGN:
Andrew Van Wart
Tatiana Loya

THE SPECIAL PEOPLE IN OUR LIVES THAT GIVE US GUIDANCE, SUPPORT, AND MUCH NEEDED HIGH FIVES:
Violette Moon Rattler, Ken Ludden, Lizbeth Davis, Amy Rosenoff, Cori Griffin.

THE MUSLIM EDITION SUPPORT TEAM:
Dawood, Hafsah, Maryam, Lena, and Hope Yasin, Asiyah, and Hadiyah Abdul-Mu'min, Rahma Zaga, Shannon Staloch, Halima Afi, and AbdulRaheem McLagan.

To find out about training to become a Cornerstone Method Childbirth Educator or a doula, please visit www.cornerstonedoulatrainings.com or www.cornerstonecbe.com.

ANY LAST NOTES:

55795732R00095

Made in the USA
San Bernardino, CA
05 November 2017